So, You Think You Know New Hampshire?

People, Places, Folklore, and Treasures

Omni Publishing Co.

2023

Todd Wiley

Published by Omni Publishing Co.
www.omni-pub.com

Cover Design: Dave Derby
www.DerbyCreative.com

Library of Congress cataloging in publication data
Wiley, Todd

So, You Think You Know New Hampshire?
People, Places, Folklore, and Treasures

ISBN: 978-1-928758-11-2

TABLE OF CONTENTS

INTRODUCTION 5

BELKNAP COUNTY 7

    Laconia 8

    Meredith 10

    Gilmanton 12

    Franconia 14

CARROLL COUNTY 19

    Wolfeboro 20

    Conway 23

    Moultonborough 25

    Sandwich 28

CHESHIRE COUNTY 31

    Keene 32

    Dublin 36

    Walpole 40

    Jaffrey 42

COOS COUNTY 45

    Berlin 46

    Dixville Notch 49

    Stark 50

    Pittsburg 51

    Gorham 53

GRAFTON COUNTY 55

    Hanover 56

    Littleton 58

    Plymouth 60

    Waterville Valley 62

    Woodsville 64

HILLSBOROUGH COUNTY 65

    Manchester 66

    Nashua..69

    Milford..73

    Peterborough 76

    Merrimack 79

MERRIMACK COUNTY 83

    Concord 84

    Canterbury...86

    Wilmot..88

    New London 89

    Loudon..91

    Henniker 92

ROCKINGHAM COUNTY 95

    Portsmouth 96

    Exeter 101

    Salem...105

    Derry..107

    Hampton..111

    Rye...114

    Seabrook...116

STRAFFORD COUNTY.. 119

    Dover..120

    Durham..124

    Rochester 127

    Lee 130

SULLIVAN COUNTY... 133

    Sunapee..134

    Claremont..136

    Newport 138

TREASURES OF NEW HAMPSHIRE 141

PHOTOS - QUESTIONS AND ANSWERS 147

INTRODUCTION

New Hampshire is known as the "Granite State," and its motto, "Live Free or Die" was coined in 1809. New Hampshire is made up of ten counties, each with its own history and unique points of interest. It was admitted to the union as the ninth state in June, 1788, and its motto, "Live Free or Die" reflects its early role in the American Revolution. Often seen as a vacation destination, it has thirteen miles of Atlantic Coastline, 300 lakes, 160 miles of the Appalachian Trail, and its highest peak is Mount Washington (6,288ft.), which once held the record for the highest wind gust at a brutal 231mph. New Hampshire is the fifth smallest state by area, and the tenth least populous state, with slightly over 1.3 million residents. Its nickname, "The Granite State," refers to its extensive granite formations and quarries.

New Hampshire has a tradition of holding the first presidential primary in the nation. Since 1960, Dixville Notch, a remote village in the White Mountains, has been the first town in the nation to vote in presidential elections. Its 29 voters gather at midnight on Primary Election Day to cast and count the ballots.

New Hampshire was inhabited for thousands of years by the Algonquian-speaking people such as the Abenaki. Europeans arrived early in the 17th century, with the English establishing some of the earliest non-indigenous settlements. The Province of New Hampshire was established in 1629, and named after the English county of Hampshire. New Hampshire saw one of the earliest overt acts of rebellion, with the seizing of Fort William and Mary from the British in 1774, and two years later became the first of the British North American colonies to establish an independent government and state constitution. In June, 1788, it was the ninth state to ratify the U.S. Constitution, bringing that document into effect.

Through the mid-19th century, New Hampshire was an active center of abolitionism, fielding close to 32,000 men for the Union during the U.S. Civil War. After the war, the state saw rapid industrialization and population growth, becoming a center of textile manufacturing, shoe-making, and paper making, and at one time home to the largest cotton textile plant in the world.

In the 21st century, New Hampshire is one of the wealthiest states in the union, with the 17th highest median household income and some of the lowest rates of poverty, unemployment, and crime. It is only one of nine states without an income tax, and has no taxes on sales, capital gains, or inheritance.

With its mountainous and heavily forested terrain, New Hampshire has a growing tourism sector centered on outdoor recreation of all kinds.

ABOUT THE AUTHOR

TODD WILEY

After spending many of my early summers along the shores of Lake Winnipesaukee and the trails of the Ossipee and White Mountains, my wife and I moved to New Hampshire in 1980, where I taught English for thirty-six years, and raised a family of three sons.

BELKNAP COUNTY

Belknap County is located slightly southeast of the state's geographic center. Its county seat is Laconia. Its total land area is 470 square miles, with 68.2 square miles as water, and is the second smallest county in New Hampshire by area. Most of the county's water area is part of Lake Winnipesaukee. As of the 2020 census, there were 56,325 people living in the county-about 140 people per square mile.

Belknap County was organized in 1840, and is named for Dr. Jeremy Belknap, a renowned preacher, historian, and author of The History of New Hampshire. There are ten towns and one city in Belknap County.

LACONIA

ALL ABOUT LACONIA

With a population of 16,871 at the 2020 census, Laconia is the county seat of Belknap County situated between Lake Winnipesaukee and Lake Winnisquam. Each June, the city hosts Laconia Motorcycle Week, more simply known as "bike week", one of the country's largest rallies. Laconia is named after the Greek region of Laconia in the southeast part of the Peloponnese peninsula.

A large Abenaki settlement once existed at the point now known as The Weirs, named by the colonists for fishing weirs. Early explorers hoped to follow the Piscataqua River north to Lake Champlain in search of the great lakes mentioned in Indian folklore. A fort was built at Laconia in 1746, but ongoing hostilities between the English, French, and respective Native American allies prevented settlement until 1761.

Beginning in 1765, lumber and grist mills were established on Mill Street, with taverns built soon after. About 1822, the courthouse was built, which would become the county seat at the creation of Belknap County in 1840. Local industry produced lumber, textiles, shoes, hosiery, knitting machinery and needles. The city's largest employer would be the Laconia Car Company, builder of rail, trolley, and subway cars. Started in1848, it lasted until the 1930s. The railroad entered town in 1849, carrying both freight and an increasing number of summer tourists to Weirs Beach. Laconia was incorporated as a city in 1893.

PEOPLE OF SIGNIFICANCE – LACONIA

Penny Pitou (b.1938) is a former United States Olympic skier, who in 1960 became the first American skier to win a medal in the Olympic downhill event. In 2001, she was inducted into the New England Women's Sports Hall of Fame. As a freshman at Laconia High, she tried out and made the boys ski team. At seventeen, she was first selected for the U.S. Olympic Ski Team. In 1960, Pitou won silver medals in both the Downhill and Giant Slalom events in Squaw Valley, California.

Doris "Granny D" Haddock (born Ethel Doris Rollins, 1910) was an American political activist, who achieved national fame when between the ages of 88 and 90 she walked over 3,200 miles across the United States to advocate for campaign finance reform. Rollins was born in Laconia, and in 1960 began her political activism when she and her husband campaigned against planned hydrogen bomb nuclear testing in Alaska. She celebrated her 100th birthday in 2010, and died six weeks later at her son's home in Dublin, New Hampshire. In 2000, Granny D received a special Martin Luther King Award; she was the keynote speaker for that year's Martin Luther King Day Community Celebration in Manchester.

Werner Doehner (b. 1929) was a German-born Mexican and American electrical engineer, and last living survivor of the Hindenburg disaster on MAY 6, 1937. He retired from New England Electric System in Westborough, Massachusetts in 1999, and moved to Laconia in 2018. He died of complications of pneumonia in 2019, at the age of 90.

DO YOU KNOW LACONIA?

Funspot Family Fun Center is an arcade that features one of the largest collections in the world of 1970s to mid-1980s games. It is located in the village of Weirs Beach in Laconia. It was officially named the "Largest Arcade in the World" by Guinness World Records in 2008. Funspot originally opened in 1952 as the Weirs Sports Center.

Weirs Beach is located on the southern shore of Lake Winnipesaukee, and the cruise ship Mount Washington terminates there. There are four marinas in the village for boat rentals, sales, and storage, and a large public dock for boaters on Lake Winnipesaukee. The Weirs Beach also contains the Winnipesaukee Playhouse, Funspot, the Winnipesaukee Scenic Railroad, Weirs Drive-in Theater, and several motels, cottage complexes, and condominiums.

Robbie Mills Field is a baseball venue in Laconia, home to the Winnipesaukee Muskrats of the collegiate summer New England Collegiate Baseball League. The field was built in 2005, and has a seating capacity of 1,200 spectators.

The **Belknap-Sulloway Mill**, now the Belknap Mill Museum is a historic mill built sometime between 1823 and 1828. It is a rare, well-preserved example of an early rural textile mill, active until 1969. It was listed on the National Register of Historic Places in 1971.

Laconia Motorcycle Week is one of the largest rallies in the world. Founded in 1923, it takes place during nine days in June, ending on Father's Day. In 2004, attendance was 375,000. Events include races, shows, and a motorcycle hill climb.

"Past Tense" is a popular Jack Reacher novel, written by Lee Childs, set in and around Laconia. The book was released in 2018.

The **Colonial Theater Complex** is a group of historic buildings in Laconia. There are three sections to the complex, but the main entrance to the theater is distinguished by a large marquee spelling out "Colonial." The complex was built in 1914, and added to the National Register of Historic Places in 2020.

The **WOW Trail** is a paved, 10 foot wide, multi-use rail trail enjoyed by bikers, walkers and runners of all ages. Built within the State of New Hampshire owned railroad right-of-way, alongside the active tracks currently leased to the Winnipesaukee Scenic Railroad, the trail currently spans from Elm Street in Lakeport to downtown Laconia and then on to the Belmont town line where it meets with Belmont's Winnisquam Scenic Trail, creating 4.25 miles of continuous trail between Lakeport and Belmont's Osborne's Agway.

MEREDITH

ALL ABOUT MEREDITH

Meredith is a 54.6 square mile town in Belknap County situated in the Lakes Region and serves as a major resort town. Its population was 6,662 at the 2020 census, and Meredith Village, the commercial center, lies along the shores of Lake Winnipesaukee. It is home to the Stonedam Island Natural Area and the Winnipesaukee Scenic Railroad and serves as one of the ports of call for the paddle steamer MS Mount Washington.

Meredith was first known as "Palmer's Town" in honor of Samuel Palmer, a teacher of surveying and navigation who laid out much of the land surrounding Lake Winnipesaukee. In 1748, it was one of the first towns to have a charter. It was settled in 1766 by Jacob Eaton and

Colonel Ebenezer Smith, then re-granted in 1768 by Governor John Wentworth and named after Sir William Meredith, 3rd Baronet, a member of Parliament who opposed taxation on the colonies.

By 1859, Meredith Village had a gristmill, sawmill, shingle mill, blacksmith shop, harness maker's shop, and tannery. Connected by the Boston, Concord & Montreal Railroad in 1849, the town became a summer resort, and remains a popular tourist destination.

PEOPLE OF SIGNIFICANCE – MEREDITH

Bradford Anderson (b. 1979) is an American actor best known for his role as the young hacker criminal on the television soap opera General Hospital. Born in Meredith, his mother worked at local theater companies and encouraged him to get involved in acting. He attended the Tisch School of Performing Arts at New York University, and while with the Philadelphia Theater Company, won an award as Best Supporting Actor for his role as Bill in Edward Albee's The Goat…Or Who is Sylvia?"

Robert William Montana (b.1920) was an American comic strip artist who created the original likeness for the characters published by Archie Comics, and in the newspaper strip Archie. Montana drew the Archie Comic strip, doing both the daily and Sunday strip for 35 years. It ran in over 750 newspapers. Montana died in 1975 of an apparent heart attack while cross-country skiing near his home in Meredith.

Barbara Annalee Davis (b.1915) moved to Meredith shortly after her marriage to Charles "Chip" Thorndike. There, she manufactured collectible "Annalee" dolls. At its height, the company filled over fourteen acres of land, with 300 employees and $15 million dollars in sales. Annalee Thornton died April 7, 2002.

DO YOU KNOW MEREDITH?

Bear Island is the second largest of the 264 islands in Lake Winnipesaukee. It was annexed by the town of Meredith in 1799, and in the summer can only be reached by boat. The island is three miles in length with about 8.5 miles of shoreline. The island is approximately 780 acres, and contains around 200 residences along the shoreline.

The **Winnipesaukee Playhouse** is a 200+ seat courtyard-style theater in Meredith. The Playhouse produces both a professional summer stock season and a community theater season. It has been the recipient of 46 New Hampshire Theater Awards over the past eight years.

Annalee Dolls, Inc. is a company located in Meredith that manufactures collectible dolls. The dolls are bendable felt-bodied dolls, with a painted face that is similar to its creator, Annalee Thorndike. By the 1960s, the dolls were being sold in stores in 40 states, Canada, and Puerto Rico. In 2008, The Winnipesaukee Playhouse purchased the former Annalee Dolls factory in Meredith.

Hart's Turkey Farm is a restaurant that has a large menu showcasing turkey dishes. It was opened in 1954. During the summer, the restaurant has 230 employees, and the restaurant sponsors an annual Thanksgiving dinner providing complimentary meals for families and individuals in need of celebrating the holiday alone. As of 2011, the restaurant sold over a ton of turkey, 1,000 pounds of potatoes, 4,000 bread rolls, 40 gallons of gravy, and 1,000 pies daily.

Lakes Region Symphony Orchestra is a non-profit community organization that provides classical and "pops" performances, held at the Inter-Lakes Community Auditorium at Inter-Lakes High School in Meredith. Musicians come from all over New Hampshire.

GILMANTON

ALL ABOUT GILMANTON

Gilmanton is a town in Belknap County that became well known in the 1950s after it was rumored that the popular novel Peyton Place, written by resident Grace Metalious, was based on the town.

Gilmanton was incorporated in 1727. First known as "Gilmantown", the town was home to the Gilman family, originally settled in Exeter. Twenty-four members of the Gilman family received grants in the new town of Gilmanton. At one time it was the second largest town in the state, following Portsmouth. The town has a total area of 59.6 square miles, and a population as of 2020 of 3,945. Its highest point is Mount Mack, at 1,945 feet above sea level.

PEOPLE OF SIGNIFICANCE - GILMANTON

John B. Bachelder (b. 1825) was a portrait and landscape painter, lithographer, and photographer, best known as the preeminent 19th-century historian of the Battle of Gettysburg in the American Civil War. Born in Gilmanton, he eventually moved to Reading, Pennsylvania, to work at a school that was to become the Pennsylvania Military Academy. From 1883 to 1887 he served as the Superintendent of Tablets and Legends for the Gettysburg Battlefield Memorial Association, and is probably responsible more than any man for the placement of monuments and battlefield markers, both Union and Confederate.

Herman Webster Mudgett, aka H.H. Holmes, (b. 1861) was an American con artist and serial killer, the subject of more than 50 lawsuits in Chicago alone. Mudgett was born in Gilmanton into a family of devout Methodists, descended from some of the first English settlers in the area. At 16 he graduated from Phillips Exeter Academy, and took a teaching job in nearby Alton. He was guilty of killing one victim, though he's suspected of killing nine. His span of crimes went from 1891-1894. On May 7, 1896, Mudgett was hanged at the Philadelphia County Prison.

Ainsworth Rand Spofford (b. 1825) was an American journalist and the sixth Librarian of Congress, serving from 1864 to 1897 under the administration of 10 presidents. Spofford was born in Gilmanton. While in Washington, shortly after reporting on the First Battle of Bull Run, he accepted a position of Chief Assistant Librarian of Congress, and later was promoted by Abraham Lincoln to Librarian of Congress.

DO YOU KNOW GILMANTON?

Crystal Lake is a 455-acre body of water in the town of Gilmanton. The shoreline along Crystal Lake consists primarily of summer cottages, with a few year-round residences. Early settlers referred to the lake as Lougee's Pond, in reference to the Lougee family that resided on the western side of the lake. Iron content in and around the lake attracted interest in iron mining that dates back to 1778. The settlement that grew up at the outlet of Crystal Lake is accordingly called Gilmanton Iron Works.

Gilmanton Academy is an historic school building built in 1894. It is a well-preserved example of a 19th-century academy building, and was one of the last to be built in the state. Today, the building houses town offices and the local historical society. It was listed on the National Register of Historic Places in 1983.

Built around 1840, the **Smith Meeting House** in Gilmanton was named for Gilmanton's first minister, Isaac Smith. The main chamber is relatively unadorned, with pine floors and wainscoting, and illuminated by electric fixtures, although original kerosene sconces and chandeliers are still present. The building was listed in the National Register of Historic Places in 1998.

The **Carpenter Museum of Antique Outboard Motors** in Gilmanton traces the history of outboard motor-boating and associated memorabilia.

The **Gilmanton Historical Society**, founded in 1967, has been committed to celebrating and preserving the history of the area. Each summer the Society hosts a number of programs that bring history to Gilmanton.

Gilmanton Winery has just about nine acres and 700 or so grapevines in Gilmanton. The winery is in the house where Grace Metalious, author of Peyton Place, lived, and is open all year.

Griswold Scout Reservation is a 3,500-acre reservation for Scouting near Gilmanton Iron Works. In 2016, the Griswold Scout Reservation and the Daniel Webster Council were awarded the "2016 Outstanding Community Tree Farmer of the Year", for exemplifying sound forest management and long-term forest management.

FRANCONIA

ALL ABOUT FRANCONIA

Franconia is home to the northern half of Franconia Notch State Park. Parts of the White Mountain National Forest are in the eastern and southern parts of the town, and the he Appalachian Trail crosses the town.

The town was first granted in 1764 by colonial governor Benning Wentworth, as "Franconia", a name widely applied to the town by 1760 due to the terrain's resemblance to the Franconian Switzerland in the region of Franconia, Germany. The town sits on a rich iron deposit, and the region once produced pig iron and bar iron for farm tools and cast iron ware.

Franconia is home to the Mountain Aerial Tramway, which rises to the 4,100-foot summit of Cannon Mountain. Built in 1938, it was the first passenger aerial tramway in North America, and from the time of its construction in 1938 to its retirement in 1980, the original tramway carried 6,581,338 passengers to the summit of Cannon Mountain.

The town has a population of 1,083 as of 2020, and a total area of 65.8 square miles. It is well known for its natural features, including Profile Lake, the Basin, Mount Lafayette, Mount Lincoln, and Cannon Mountain. Mount Lafayette is the highest peak in Franconia and in Grafton County, as well as the second most prominent peak in the White Mountains, after Mount Washington.

PEOPLE OF SIGNIFICANCE - FRANCONIA

Samuel "Bode" Miller (b.1977) is an American former World Cup Alpine ski racer. He is an Olympic and World Championship gold medalist, a two-time overall World Cup champion in 2005 and 2008, and is the most successful male American alpine ski racer of all time. He is also considered one of the greatest World Cup racers of all time with 33 race victories. In 2008, Miller and Lindsey Vonn won the overall World Cup titles for the first U.S. sweep in 25 years. Miller grew up in Franconia in the heart of New Hampshire's White Mountains.

Jessica Garretson Finch (b. 1871) was an American educator, author, women's rights activist, Founder of the Lennox School for girls, and founding president of Finch College. Her family moved to Franconia when she was twelve, and she attended Dow Academy and the Cambridge Latin School before entering Barnard College. She applied to law school at Columbia University, but was turned down on the grounds that the Law School didn't accept women. She did, however, earn her LL.B from New York University Law School in 1898. She was a well-known suffragette, and an advocate for careers for women.

Selden Hanna (b.1913) was an intercollegiate, U.S. F.I.S., and seniors ski champion who became one of the nation's most prolific ski-area architects. He was enshrined in the National Ski Hall of Fame in 1968.

His legacy remains throughout New England and North America in more than 250 ski area with witch he was associated during his lifetime. He died in Franconia on August 31, 1991.

Do You Know Franconia?

Around 1940, actress **Bette Davis** vacationed in the town bordering Franconia, when she got lost in the woods. Arthur Farnsworth, who worked at Peckett's Ski School, found her and rescued her from the woods. They fell in love and soon married. Farnsworth died unexpectedly, and Davis erected a rock on the BRIDAL VEIL FALLS with the inscription: "The Keeper of Stray Ladies."

In addition to the mountains around **Franconia Notch**, there are several other four-thousand-footers within the town limits: Mount Garfield, Galehead Mountain, South Twin Mountain, and Owl's Head.

The **Frost Place** is an educational center for poetry located on Robert Frost's former home on Ridge Road in Franconia. The façade offers a fine view of the Franconia Range and Mount Lafayette. The Frost family lived in the house until 1920, and spent their summers there for nearly twenty years. The property was listed on the National Register of Historic Places in 1976.

Founded in 1977, **The New England Ski Museum** is situated near the Tramway of Cannon Mountain ski area, in Franconia Notch State Park. The museum was designed to preserve the history of commercial and recreational skiing, both alpine and cross-country, in the northeastern United States.

Franconia Notch State Park is a public recreation area and nature preserve that passes through Franconia Notch, a mountain pass between the Kinsman Range and Franconia Range in the White Mountains of northern New Hampshire. Attractions include the Flume Gorge and Visitor's Center, the Old Man in the Mountain historical site, fishing in Echo Lake and Profile Lake, and miles of hiking, biking and ski trails. It also boasts an aerial tram which runs year-round, ferrying sightseers to the summit in the summer, and skiers in the winter.

Cannon Mountain Ski Area is a state-owned ski resort located on Cannon Mountain in the White Mountains, and boasts the first aerial tramway in North America. Cannon is the most vertical of any ski area in New Hampshire at 2,180 feet, and is the seventh largest in New England. The mountain offers 10 lifts servicing 265 acres of skiing (168 with snowmaking), and 23 miles of trails.

Profile House was a grand hotel in the White Mountains, built in 1852. The hotel was named for the iconic rock structure discovered by surveyors in 1805 that came to be known as the "Old Man in the Mountain". The Profile House in Franconia Notch existed for 70 years. The first Profile House opened in 1853, and the "New" Profile burned in 1923. At the time of its destruction, it could accommodate 600 guests and was the most luxurious hotel on the west side of the mountains. The hotel operated a large farm, greenhouse, bowling alley, billiard hall, barber shop, music room, golf course, telegraph office, trout pond and fish hatchery. Today, the parking lot for the Cannon Mountain Ski Area and Tramway is located just north of the site where the hotel once stood.

CAN YOU IDENTIFY THIS PHOTO? The Memorial Arch of Tilton, sometimes referred to as Tilton's Folly, is a historic arch on Elm Street in Northfield on a hill overlooking the town of Tilton. The 55-foot-tall arch was built by Charles E. Tilton in 1882; it was modeled after the Arch of Titus in Rome. The Memorial Arch of Tilton was added to the National Register of Historic Places in 1980.

WHERE DID THIS SAYING ORIGINATE? Live Free or Die was part of a toast that was to be made at an anniversary reunion by General John Stark who missed the event.

CARROLL COUNTY

Carroll County is the third least populated county in New Hampshire, with a population of 50,107 as of 2020. Its county seat is Ossipee, and it is named in honor of Charles Carroll of Carrollton, who died in 1832, the last surviving signer of the United States Declaration of Independence. The county was created in 1840, and has a total area of 992 square miles making it the third largest county in New Hampshire by total area. The county is historically Republican, but in 2008 Barack Obama received 52.3% of the county's vote, making it the first Democratic presidential nominee to win the county since 1912, and the first Democratic presidential nominee to win an absolute majority in the county since 1884. Northern Carroll County is known for being quite mountainous, and Cranmore Mountain, Attitash, King Pine, and Black Mountain ski areas are located here.

WOLFEBORO

ALL ABOUT WOLFEBORO

Wolfeboro was granted by colonial Governor Benning Wentworth in 1759 to four young men of Portsmouth and named "Wolfeboro" in honor of English General James Wolfe, who was victorious at the Battle of the Plains of Abraham during the French and Indian War. Benning Wentworth's nephew established an estate on the site, known as Kingswood. Built in 1771 beside what is now known as Lake Wentworth, this was the first summer country estate in northern New England. Settled in 1768, the town was incorporated in 1770. Over the years Wolfeboro, whose motto is "The Oldest Summer Resort in America", has become a popular summer colony.

The main village of Wolfeboro is located at the head of Wolfeboro Bay on Lake Winnipesaukee, and has a total area of 58.5 square miles, 48.0 of which are land, and 10.5 square miles are water. As of the 2020 census, the town's population was 6,416, and the highest point in town is Moody Mountain, with an elevation of 1,420 feet above sea level.

PEOPLE OF SIGNIFICANCE - WOLFEBORO

James Foley (b.1973) was an American journalist. While working as a freelance war correspondent during the Syrian Civil War, he was abducted and murdered in August, 2014 purportedly as a response to American airstrikes in Iraq, thus becoming the first American citizen killed by the Islamic State of Iraq and Syria (ISIS). The James W. Foley Legacy Foundation was established following his death. He grew up in Wolfeboro, where he attended Kingswood Regional High School.

Jeb Bradley (b.1952) is an American politician who serves in the New Hampshire Senate. He represents his hometown of Wolfeboro and 16 towns in east-central New Hampshire for District 3. Bradley is an avid hiker who has ascended all of New Hampshire's forty-eight 4,000-foot peaks, and is a member of the Appalachian Mountain-Club's Four Thousand Footer Club. Bradley lives in Wolfeboro.

Robbie Ftorek (b.1952) is an American professional ice hockey coach and former player. He was enshrined as a member of the United States Hockey Hall of Fame in 1991. He played on the 1972 United States Olympic Hockey team that won the silver medal at the 1972 Winter Olympics. Ftorek and his wife have four children, and live in Wolfeboro.

Willard "Mitt" Romney (b. 1947) is an American politician, businessman, and lawyer serving as the junior United States senator from Utah. He served as the 70th governor of Massachusetts from 2003 to 2007, and was the Republican Party's nominee for president of the United States in the 2012 election. The Romneys own an estate along Lake Winnipesaukee in Wolfeboro.

Do You Know Wolfeboro?

Lake Winnipesaukee is the largest lake in New Hampshire, located in the Lakes Region at the foothills of the White Mountains. The Abenaki name, Winnipesaukee means either "smile of the great spirit" or "beautiful water in a high place." The lake is approximately 21 miles long, and from 1 to 9 miles wide, covering 69 square miles and a maximum depth of 180 feet. The center of the lake is called The Broads. The lake contains at least 264 islands, and is the third-largest lake in New England after Lake Champlain and Moosehead Lake. Lake Winnipesaukee has been a popular tourist destination for more than a century. Since records began in 1851, ice-out has happened as early as March 18, and as late as May 12, although 90 percent of the time it's declared during April.

Lake Winnipesaukee Mystery Stone is an alleged out-of-place artifact found in a town near the lake. The stone's age, purpose and origin are unknown. The stone is about 4 inches long and 2.5 inches thick, dark and egg shaped, bearing a variety of carved symbols. The stone was reportedly found in 1872, and is currently on exhibit at the Museum of New Hampshire History.

Libby Museum is a natural history museum in Wolfeboro. Founded in 1912 by Dr. Henry Libby, it was the first museum in the state dedicated solely to its natural history. The museum includes specimens of plants, animals, birds, and fish, as well as minerals, and is opened seasonally between June and Columbus Day weekend in October.

Pickering House is an historic house in Wolfeboro, dating back to 1813, and built by Daniel Pickering, the town's first postmaster. The property was listed on the National Register of Historic Places in 2019, and has since been turned into a boutique hotel that opened in 2018.

Brewster Academy is a coeducational independent boarding school on 80 acres in Wolfeboro, serving around 350 students. The school was founded in 1820, and in 1887 was renamed "Brewster Free Academy" in honor of benefactor John Brewster. In 2020, Brewster's prep basketball team won their 7th National Prep Basketball Championship, and eighteen alumni have played in the NBA.

The **MS Mount Washington** is the flagship vessel of the Winnipesaukee Flagship Corporation, making several ports of call around the lake during the spring, summer, and fall months. The Mount Washington has five ports of call: Meredith Bay, Center Harbor, Wolfeboro, Alton Bay, and Weirs Beach. The original paddle steamer Mount Washington was launched in 1872, and in 2021 the **Winnipesaukee Spirit** was added to the fleet, equipped with its own bar and galley area with indoor/outdoor seating as well as two lounge areas.

The **New Hampshire Boat Museum** was founded in 1922 by a group of antique and classic boating enthusiasts who wanted to preserve the boating heritage on New Hampshire's waterways, and for the past 22 years it has had its home in Wolfeboro. In addition to a number of displays, classes, educational programs, model boat building, and an annual boat show, visitors can also experience the thrill of riding in a replica vintage boat.

The **Wright Museum of World War 2** accomplishes its mission through careful preservation and thoughtful display of its extensive permanent collection of 1939 – 1945 items; thereby building a reputation as a national repository for historically significant WWII items and memorabilia. Unique to traditional WWII museums, the over 14,000 items in its collection are representative of both the home front and the battlefield. These irreplaceable items, together with fully operational military vehicles, introduce visitors to a seminal period in American history.

CONWAY

ALL ABOUT CONWAY

Conway is the most populous community in the county with a population of 9,822 at the 2020 census. The town is on the southeastern edge of the White Mountain National Forest and serves as the main economic hub for Carroll County. Tourism is a principal business

In 1765, colonial Governor Benning Wentworth chartered 65 men to establish "Conway", named for Henry Seymour Conway, who was later named Commander in Chief of the British Army. The first roads were built in 1766, and by 1775 the town raised funds to build two schoolhouses. By 1849, however, the town had 20 school districts. The town has a total area of 71.7 square miles, and its highest peak is Black Cap, rising 2,369 feet above sea level. With the arrival of the railway in 1871, numerous inns and taverns were built as tourism flourished. The first ski trail began operating in 1936, and in 1959, the Kancamagus Highway opened connecting Conway with Lincoln.

PEOPLE OF SIGNIFICANCE – CONWAY

Sean Doherty (b.1995) is an American biathlete born in Conway. Doherty competed in the 2014 Winter Olympics in Sochi, Russia, and in the 2018 Winter Olympics in Pyeongchang, South Korea. He competed in the Biathlon World Cup opening 2015 in Ostersund, Jamtland, Sweden, and represented the United States at the 2022 Winter Olympics.

Donald Philbrick (b.1937) was an American politician. He was born in Conway, graduated from Kennett High School, served in the United States Air Force from 1954 to 1976, and then served in the New Hampshire House of Representatives for 14 years.

James Farrington (b.1791) was an American physician, banker, and politician. He served as a member of the United States House of Representatives, the New Hampshire Senate, and the New Hampshire House of Representatives in the early 1800s. He attended the common schools in Conway, graduated from Fryeburg Academy in 1814, studied medicine and began to practice medicine in 1818. He was a member of the NH Medical Society, and after leaving congress was appointed one of the trustees of the New Hampshire Insane Asylum.

Do You Know Conway?

Echo Lake State Park is a public recreation area that features 15.7-acre Echo Lake and Cathedral Ledge and Whitehorse Ledge, two rock ledges with scenic views. There is a one-mile trail around the lake, and a mile-long auto road and hiking trails that lead to the top of Cathedral Ledge (elevation 1.159 feet). In 1899, Cathedral Ledge was purchased for $1,000 by a group of visitors and local residents, and later deeded to the State of New Hampshire.

Tuckerman Brewing Company is a brewery in Conway, named after the nearby Tuckerman Ravine. A portion of the sale of its stout goes to support the Mount Washington Observatory, which sits 6,288 feet above sea level on Mount Washington.

Conway Scenic Railway is a heritage railroad in North Conway. The railroad operates two historic routes: a line from North Conway to Conway, and a line from North Conway through Crawford Notch. The railroad's main terminal is in historic downtown North Conway in the Mount Washington Valley, and has been listed on the National Register of Historic Places since 1979.

Cranmore Mountain Resort is a ski area located in North Conway that began operations in 1937. In its early years, Cranmore distinguished itself from other ski areas by its Skimobile, a relatively developed base area and lodging, and a ski school run by European skiers. During the 1940s, Cranmore was one of the first ski areas to take an interest in trail grooming technology. In 2019, the mountain opened its ski and snowboard season on November 16, the earliest opening in resort history. Cranmore has over 200 acres of skiable terrain, with the longest run of about a mile.

Mount Washington Observatory is a private, non-profit, scientific and educational institution. The weather observation station is located on the summit of Mount Washington. The first regular meteorological observations on Mount Washington were conducted by the U.S. Signal Service, a precursor of the Weather Bureau, from 1870 to 1892. The Mount Washington station was the first of its kind in the world. On April 12, 1934, the observatory staff recorded a wind gust of 231 miles per hour, a record that was held until 1996. The Sherman Adams summit building is named for the 67th governor of New Hampshire.

Mount Washington State Park is a 63-acre parcel perched on the summit of Mount Washington, the highest peak in the northeastern United States. The land forming the park was originally given to Dartmouth College in 1951, then sold to the state of New Hampshire. In 1642, Darby Field was the first to climb to the summit of Mount Washington, supposedly with guidance by local Native Americans. Construction of the auto road began in 1854, and the current road completed building in1859. The park is open May to October.

CAN YOU IDENTIFY THESE PHOTOS? Diana's Baths, in Conway, is a series of pools and cascades on Lucy Brook about a three quarter mile walk on the Moat Mountain Trail (northern terminus). The section of the trail up to the Baths is ADA with benches along the way.

MOULTONBOROUGH

ALL ABOUT MOULTONBOROUGH

Moultonborough is a town in Carroll County with a population of 4,918 in 2020. It is bounded by Lake Winnipesaukee in the southwest, and to a lesser extent by Squam Lake in the northwest corner. The first European settlers were grantees from Hampton, New Hampshire, among whom were sixteen Moultans, giving the town its name. Moultonborough was chartered in 1763, and officially incorporated in 1777. The town has a total area of 75.1 square miles, of which 59.7 square miles are land and 15.4 square miles are water, comprising 20.50% of the town. A large portion of the town is located along Lake

Winnipesaukee, the largest lake in New Hampshire. Mount Shaw, part of the Ossipee Mountains, is the highest point at 2,990 feet.

PEOPLE OF SIGNIFICANCE - MOULTONBOROUGH

Jonathan Moulton (b.1726) spent much of his childhood as an apprentice to a cabinetmaker. He won his freedom in 1745, and worked as a silversmith, forming the Moulton and Towle Silversmithing Company, which still manufactures silverware and kitchen utensils today. During the American Revolutionary War, Colonel Moulton's regiment guarded the 18-mile seacoast of New Hampshire against British invasion. In the fall of 1777, he marched with his men to the Battle of Saratoga in New York and the defeat of Lieutenant General John Burgoyne's British Army invading from Canada. He was promoted to Brigadier General by George Washington, and was rewarded with lands in the lakes region, founding the town of Moultonborough.

Claud Rains (b. 1889) was a British actor whose career spanned seven decades. He was a Tony Award winning actor and four-time nominee for the Academy Award for Best Supporting Actor. A chronic alcoholic, Rains died of cirrhosis of the liver in 1967 and was buried at the Red Hill Cemetery in Moultonborough.

John Greenleaf Whittier (b. 1807) was an American poet and advocate of the abolition of slavery in the United States. Often listed as one of the "fireside poets", he was influenced by the Scottish poet Robert Burns. In 1833, Whittier published the antislavery pamphlet Justice and Expediency, and from there dedicated the next 20 years of his life to the abolitionist cause. He was one of the founders of the American Anti-Slavery Society, which he considered the most significant action of his life. Mount Whittier in New Hampshire is named for him. He spent summers in Moultonborough and Hampton Falls.

Thomas Gustave Plant (b.1859) was the son of French Canadian immigrants who made his fortune manufacturing shoes. Plant used his fortune to build Lucknow, now known as Castle in the Clouds, an estate on a mountain overlooking Lake Winnipesaukee in Moultonborough, where he lived with his second wife. Plant went bankrupt with the collapse of the stock exchange in 1929, but was allowed to live in his home even as they dissolved his estate.

DO YOU KNOW MOULTONBOROUGH?

Castle in the Clouds was built in 1913-1914 by the millionaire shoe manufacturer Thomas Gustav Plant, for his second wife, Olive Cornelia Dewey. It is a 16-room mansion and 5,294-acre mountaintop estate in Moultonborough, overlooking Lake Winnipesaukee and the Ossipee Mountains from a rocky outcropping known as "The Crow's Nest". The property was assembled from the private Ossipee Mountain Park, and included the mansion, a stable/garage, gatehouses, a greenhouse, farm buildings, and a golf course - eventually extending to 6,000 acres. Today, the Castle in the Clouds is owned and operated by the Castle Preservation Society. It was listed on the National Register of Historic Places in 2018.

CAN YOU IDENTIFY THIS PHOTO? Castle in the Clouds in Moultonborough New Hampshire.

Geneva Point Center is an historic summer camp and conference center in Moultonborough. Founded in 1919, the center is located on 184 acres and holds conferences, camp groups, family groups, and other events. The complex includes historic buildings including the Winnipesaukee Inn, converted in1896 and previously the grand barn of a chicken farm. The Moultonborough Town House, the former town hall built in 1834, was listed on the National Register of Historic Places in 1989, and the NH State Register of Historic Places in 2004.

SANDWICH

ALL ABOUT SANDWICH

Chartered in 1763, Sandwich is part of the White Mountain National Forest in the north, and part of Squam Lake in the southwest corner of town. The land was considered so inaccessible that the grant was enlarged, making Sandwich on of the largest towns in the state. It was named in honor of John Montagu, 4th Earl of Sandwich, said to be the inventor of the sandwich.

The earliest European settlers arrived in 1767, and by 1830 the town had grown to a population of 2,700, nearly double the current population of 1,466 (2020). At that time the town contained farms, stores, mills churches schools, carpenters, blacksmiths, and wheelwrights. By the end of the 1800s, much of the population left for the cities, and Sandwich became an attraction for visitors, summer residents and artists.

PEOPLE OF SIGNIFICANCE - SANDWICH

Dixi Crosby (b.1800), born in Sandwich, was an American surgeon and educator at Dartmouth College. Crosby created a new technique for reducing metacarpophalangeal dislocation, and was the first surgeon to open an abscess at the hip joint. He was also the first surgeon in the U.S. to be sued for medical malpractice. Crosby received his degree from Dartmouth Medical School in 1824. He served in the provost marshal's office during the Civil War, and was given an honorary doctor's degree of LL.D by Dartmouth in 1867. He retired in 1870.

Norbert Wiener (b.1894) was a professor of mathematics at the Massachusetts Institute of Technology. Wiener became an early researcher in electronic engineering, electronic communication, and control systems. At 11 years of age Wiener entered Tufts College, graduating at the age of 14 with a BA in mathematics, then to Harvard for studies in zoology. In 1910 he transferred to Cornell to study philosophy, where he graduated in 1911 at the age of 17. Wiener died in 1964, and is buried at the Vittum Hill Cemetery in Sandwich.

Isaac Adams (b. 1802) was an American inventor and politician who invented the Adams power press, which revolutionized the printing industry. At an early age he worked in a cotton factory, later learning the trade of cabinetmaker. In 1824 he went to Boston and sought work in a machine shop. In 1828 he invented the Adams printing press, and by 1836 it became the leading machine used in book printing for much of the 19th century, and was distributed worldwide. It substantially reduced the cost of book production, and made books more widely available.

Do You Know Sandwich?

The **Sandwich Fair** was first held in October 1919 and celebrated its centennial in 2010 with 35,000 people attending. The annual event is held on Columbus Day weekend and includes two parades: an antique auto parade, and the "Grand Parade" on Sunday. There is a midway, animal shows, and oxen pulling, with an original Abbot-Downing Company Concord Coach leading the parade.

The **League of New Hampshire Craftsmen** began in Sandwich as "Sandwich Home Industries" in 1920, and continues statewide today. The **Center Sandwich Fine Art Gallery** was a founding member of the League of New Hampshire Craftsmen, and has been supporting artisans and craft education for over 90 years.

Durgin Bridge is a covered bridge over the Cold River in Sandwich. Built in 1869, it is a rare surviving example of a Paddleford truss bridge, and one of the few surviving 19th-century covered bridges in New Hampshire and Sandwich's only surviving 19th-century covered bridge.

Squam Lake straddles the borders of Carroll, Grafton, and Belknap counties; covering 6,791 acres, it is the second largest lake located entirely in New Hampshire. Squam Lake is a nesting site for common loons as well as Bald eagles and great blue herons. The 1981 film On Golden Pond, starring Katharine Hepburn, Henry Fonda and Jane Fonda, was filmed in the town of Center Harbor on Squam Lake, which is much less commercialized than its neighbor, Lake Winnipesaukee.

Chapman Sanctuary and **Visny Woods** is 160 acres of woodlands and meadow open to the public for recreational use. There are 10 miles of trails, including a self-guided nature trail that is home to a variety of birds and other wildlife. There is no admission fee, and it is also open for cross-country skiing and snowshoeing.

CAN YOU IDENTIFY THIS PHOTO? The Zimmerman House was designed by Frank Lloyd Wright and is owned by the Currier museum

CHESHIRE COUNTY

Cheshire County is in the southwest portion of New Hampshire, and as of 2020 has a population of 76,458. Cheshire was one of the five original counties of New Hampshire, and is named for the county of Cheshire in England. It was organized in 1771 at Keene, which is the county seat. Sullivan County was created from the northern portion of Cheshire County in1827. The county has an area of 729 square miles, with its highest point being Mt. Monadnock in the northwest part of Jaffrey, at 3,165 feet. There are 154 properties and districts on the National Register of Historic Places in Cheshire County, including one National Historic Landmark.

KEENE

ALL ABOUT KEENE

Keene is a city in and is the seat of Cheshire County. Its population was 23,047 at the 2020 census. In 1735, Governor Jonathan Belcher granted lots in the township of "Upper Ashuelot" to sixty-three settlers. Settled after 1736, it was intended to be a fort town protecting the Province of Massachusetts Bay from the French and their Native allies during the French and Indian Wars. When the boundary between The Massachusetts Bay and New Hampshire colonies was fixed in 1741, Upper Ashuelot became part of New Hampshire, although Massachusetts continued supporting the area for its own protection.

In1747, during Kin George's War, the village was attacked and burned by Natives, but was rebuilt in 1749. It was granted to its inhabitants in 1753 by Governor Benning Wentworth who renamed it "Keene" after Sir Benjamin Keene, English Minister to Spain, and a West Indies trader. Located in the center of Cheshire County, Keene was designated as the county seat in1769.

After the railroad was constructed in1848, numerous industries were established, and Keene became a manufacturing center for woodenware, pails, chairs, shutters, doors, pottery, glass, soap, woolen textiles, saddles, carriages and sleighs. It also had a brickyard and foundry, and by 1880 had a population of 6,748. In the early 1900s, the Newburyport Silver Company moved to Keene to take advantage of its skilled workers and location. Keene today is a center for insurance, education, and tourism. The city retains a considerable inventory of fine Victorian architecture from its mill town era, an example of which is the Keene Public Library, which occupies a Second Empire mansion built around 1869 by manufacturer Henry Colony.

PEOPLE OF SIGNIFICANCE - KEENE

Richard B. Cohen (b. 1952) is an American billionaire and owner of C&S Wholesale Grocers, a wholesale grocery supply company, as well as chairman and chief executive of Symbiotic, an artificial intelligence-enabler robotics company. In 1989, Cohen took control of C&S after his father retired, and moved the company headquarters to Keene. Cohen is also the founder of Symbiotic, a robotics warehouse automation company, used by C&S, Walmart, Target, and other large retailers. In 2001, The Center for Holocaust Studies at Keene State College was renamed after the Cohens in thanks for their financial support.

Barry Faulkner (b. 1881) was an American artist primarily known for his murals. During World War I, he and sculptor Sherry Edmundson Fry organized artists for training as camouflage specialists, an effort that contributed to the founding of the American Camouflage Corps in 1917. Faulkner worked as a muralist from his studio in New York City, and was elected to the National Academy of Design in 1926. He continued to serve as a trustee and active member of the American Academy, and in 1960 received a Rome Medal for outstanding service. Faulkner's earliest commissions were for murals in the homes of prominent people, and those led to commissions for others:

- The Cunard Building, New York City
- University of Illinois Library, Urbana, Illinois
- RCA Building, New York City
- National Archives Building, Washington, DC
- Senate Chamber, New Hampshire State Capital
- John Hancock Building, Boston
- Mortensen Hall at Bushnell Center, Hartford, Connecticut

The center panel of the ceiling in **Mortensen Hall** is the largest hand-painted ceiling mural in the United States and cost $50,000 in 1929.

Catherine Fiske (b. 1784) was an American teacher and principal who founded a girls' boarding school, Miss Catherine Fiske's Young Ladies Seminary. Located in Keene, it was in operation from 1814 until the 1840s. Presently, the seminary's building serves as President's House, Keene State College. Fiske was also a benefactor for the New Hampshire State Hospital.

33

Fiske had been engaged in teaching for 15 years, before coming to Keene in 1911. She began teaching, but did not open Fiske's Young Ladies Seminary until 1914. She had purchased a building with a large farm, later known as the "Thayer" property. The school admitted both boarding and day scholars, and at one time, a class of boys was also admitted as day scholars. Both the school and the farm were managed by Fiske, and her vigilance never relaxed. She operated the seminary until her death in 1837, and during her 38 years as a teacher, it's estimated that she had under her care more than 2,500 pupils.

Allen George Lafley (b. 1947) is an American businessman who led consumer goods maker Proctor & Gamble from 2000 to 2010, and from 2013 to2015, during which time he served as chairman, president, and CEO, eventually retiring in 2016. Lafley is credited with revitalizing P & G with a focus on brands like Crest, Tide, and Pampers, and bringing in several new brands like Swiffer and Febreze. He studied at Harvard Business School, receiving his M.B.A. in 1977, and joined P & G upon his graduation. He has won many awards for his contributions to innovation, marketing, and human-centered design, and in 2110 was honored with an Edison Achievement award for his commitment to innovation throughout his career.

Do You Know Keene?

Keene is often considered a minor college town, as it is the site of **Keene State College**, whose 5,400 students make up over one-quarter of the city's population, and Antioch University New England. Keene State is a public liberal arts college, part of the University System of New Hampshire and the Council of Public Liberal Arts Colleges. Keene State College was founded in 1909, as a teacher's college, and currently has an enrollment of 3,104 and a campus of 150 acres. Antioch University was founded in 1852 by politician, abolitionist, and education reformer-Horace Mann, and is committed to nonsectarian, co-educational pathways to innovation and progress. Today, Antioch University, New England serves a student body of around 1,000 students, offering four certificate programs, master's degrees in twenty-three different programs, and three doctoral programs.

In popular culture, the 1949 film **"Lost Boundaries"** starring Mel Ferrer, tells the true story of a black Keene physician who passed as white for many years. The film won the 1949 Cannes Film Festival award for best screenplay.

In 1995, much of the movie **"Jumanji"**, starring Robin Williams was filmed in Keene as the movie's fictional town of Brantford. Frank's Barber Shop is a featured setting as well as the Parrish Shoe sign, which was painted for the film. The sign served as a focal point for a temporary Robin Williams memorial in the days following the actor's death in 2014.

In music, **First Lady Rosalynn Carter** dedicated the bandstand in Central Square as the E.E. Bagley Bandstand, after the noted composer of the National Emblem March, who made Keene his home until his death in 1922. Many groups perform on a regular basis, including the Keene Chamber Orchestra, the Keene Chamber Singers, the Greater Keene Pops Choir, and the Keene Jazz Orchestra.

Keene is home to the **Keene Swamp Bats** team of the New England Collegiate Baseball League. The Swamp Bats are five-time league champions, and are consistently at the top of the NECBL in attendance, and the **Monadnock Wolfpack Rugby Football Club** now calls Keene its home. They play in the New England Rugby Football Union, and will defend their undefeated championship 2018 season in the fall of 1019.

Every October from 1991 to 2014, Keene hosted an annual pumpkin festival known as **Pumpkin Fest**. The event set world records several times for the largest simultaneous number of jack-o-lanterns on display. The first time was in 1993, when Keene set the record with nearly 5,000 carved and lit pumpkins. In 2103 it again set the record with a total of 30.581 pumpkins according to the Guinness Book of Records.

Faulkner & Colony Woolen Mill was constructed in 1838, and named after Francis Faulkner and Josiah Colony who owned multiple mills along the Ashuelot River. The mill provided material or many uses, including to the U.S. Military during the Civil War, World War I, and World War II. Development in synthetic caused the mill to close in 1954, making it the longest running family-owned textile mill in the country. The property was converted to retail and office space in 1983 and was later converted to residential apartments.

The **Noah Cooke House** was built in 1791, and is one of Keene's oldest surviving buildings. This saltbox colonial listed on the National Register of Historic Places, was originally located on Main Street, but was moved to its present rural setting in 1973.

The **Stone Arch Bridge** is a stone arch railway bridge in Keene and is one of the best-preserved pre-1850 stone arch bridges in the nation. Built in 1847 to carry the Cheshire Railroad, it now carries a multipurpose rail trail. Its central feature is a massive granite arch spanning The Branch River. The arch has a span of 68 feet 9 inches, a width of 27 feet 1 inch, and a rise of about 48 feet above the typical water level. At one time, the bridge was one of the largest stone arch bridged in the nation, but was formally abandoned in 1972, an d much of its New Hampshire right of way was acquired by the state in the 1990s.

Stonewall Farm in Keene uses regenerative farming practices to enrich their soil and improve the health of their dairy herd and vegetable crops. They also strive to spread regenerative agriculture practices throughout New England by serving as a demonstration site and offering educational programs.

DUBLIN

ALL ABOUT DUBLIN

In 1749, the Masonian proprietors granted the town as "Monadnock No. 3" (or North Monadnock) to Mathew Thornton and thirty-nine others, though none of them became settlers in the township. The deed of grant was given by Col. Joseph Blanchard in 1749, but the French and Indian War thwarted permanent settlement until the 1760s when Henry Strongman moved from Peterborough. In 1771, Governor John Wentworth incorporated the town, naming it after Strongman's birthplace: Dublin, Ireland.

The town of Dublin has a total area of 29 square miles, with its highest point along the northern slopes of Mount Monadnock where the elevation reaches 2.834 feet above sea level. There are several ponds in Dublin including Monadnock Lake (now known as Dublin Pond), Farnum (Dark) Pond, and Wight Pond, as well as Howe, Knight, and Electric Company reservoirs. Dublin Pond is a clean sheet of water that has brought many families to Dublin. It's surrounded by a vast area of woods leading to the edge of the summit of Mount Monadnock, and from its surface the summit and northwest sides of the mountain are visible.

The history of Dublin's architecture starts with the foundation of the United States, and the development of the Federal Style of architecture. Dublin's style can be attributed to Rufus Piper, who served as town moderator and was a carpenter at the time. He was responsible for adding fans to various houses in the town, which included his, and his grandfather's house.

PEOPLE OF SIGNIFICANCE - DUBLIN

Greenville Clark (b. 1882) was a Wall Street lawyer, member of the Harvard Corporation, co-author of the book "World Peace through World Law", and nominee for the Nobel Peace Prize. In 1909, Clark founded a law firm, which flourished during the Depression by focusing on bankruptcy and reorganization, and New Deal regulations. The firm expanded from 8 to 74 associates, and opened a second office in Washington, D.C. while building up a corporate practice with clients such as AT&T and Standard Oil.

In 1945, Clark and several others held the "Dublin Conference" in Dublin. There they passed a "Dublin Declaration", which judging the U.N. Charter inadequate to preserve peace, proposed transformation of the U.N. General assembly into a world legislature. In 1965, Clark held a second "Dublin Conference" which made a second declaration. His amendments sought to turn the United Nations into a true world federal government. Clark, a personal friend of Teddy Roosevelt died in 1967 at his home in Dublin.

Doris Haddock (b. 1910) was an American political activist from New Hampshire. She achieved national fame when, between the ages of 88 and 90, she walked over 3,200 miles across the continental United States to advocate for campaign finance reform. Haddock's walk across the country followed a southern route and took more than a year to complete, starting on January 1, 1999 in southern California and ending in Washington, D.C. on February 29, 2000. Haddock celebrated her 100th birthday on January 24, 2010, and died six weeks later at her son's home in Dublin.

William Preston Phelps (b. 1848) was an American landscape painter, known as "the Painter of the Monadnock". He was born on the family farm in what is now called the Pottersville section of Dublin. He grew up helping on the farm, where his father in his spare time, liked to paint, build furniture and musical instruments. Phelps drew constantly, and his father recognized the financial benefits of his talents, and at age 14 sent him to Lowell, Massachusetts to work for a sign painter. In time, people were so impressed with his work, patrons started to hire him for canvas paintings, and he began taking evening art classes in Boston. After a few years, at the age of 27, he had his first exhibition of his work in Lowell, where a group of patrons were so impressed that they funded Phelps to study abroad in Munich.

After spending a majority of his 30s traveling and painting in Europe and the U.S., he settled down when he re-acquired his old family farm. He remained in the area painting many New England landscapes. Phelps died at the age of 75 in the same community he was born in. Today, many of his works are archived at the Smithsonian.

Do You Know Dublin?

Based in Dublin, **Yankee Magazine** is one of the few remaining family-owned and independent magazine publishers in the United States. The first issue appeared in 1935 and has a paid circulation of below 300,000 in 2015, from a peak of one million in the 1980s. Yankee Publishing also owns the oldest continuously produced periodical in the U.S., the Old Farmer's Almanac, which it purchased in 1939.

The Dublin School is an independent college preparatory school in Dublin. The school was founded in 1935, and has worked to provide students with abroad-based college preparatory education emphasizing community values and individual responsibility. It has a student body of 165, and has grown from approximately 110 students in 2008. Approximately 75% are boarding students. The school is located on over five hundred acres, with over 15 miles of hiking trails. In addition to traditional classrooms, specialized facilities include the Fountain Arts Building with a state of the art sound and light equipment, and an outdoor performance space for spring concerts. It also offers a high tech computer lab for digital photography and filmmaking, The Perkins Observatory, robotics labs, a music and recording studio, and a writer's cottage.

The Walden School is an organization which runs summer music education programs, the only summer program dedicated specifically to young composers in the United States. Programs take place on the campus of the Dublin School, and feature visiting professional ensembles who help to perform new music written by participants. Walden School Faculty are active composers, performers, and educators.

Mount Monadnock, in the towns of Jaffrey and Dublin, is the most prominent peak in southern New Hampshire, and the highest in Cheshire County. At 3,165 feet, Mount Monadnock is nearly 1,000 feet higher than any other mountain peak within 30 miles. Its bare, rocky summit provides expansive views, and has long been cited as one of the most frequently climbed mountains in the world. It is featured in the writings of Ralph Waldo Emerson and Henry David Thoreau.

It has a number of trails, and it is believed that the summit is barren largely because of fires set by early settlers. The first major fire, set in 1800 to clear the lower slopes for pasture, swept through the stands of virgin red spruce on the summit and flanks of the mountain. Between 1810 and 1820, local farmers, who believed that wolves were denning in the blowdowns, set fire to the mountain again. The fire raged for weeks, destroying the topsoil and denuding the mountain above 2,000 feet. The word "monadnock" is derived from an Abenaki word used to describe the mountain, and loosely translated as, "mountain that stands alone".

Ralph Waldo Emerson, Henry David Thoreau, and Margaret Fuller visited the mountain, and wrote fondly of it. Thoreau visited the mountain four times between 1844 and 1860, and spent a great deal of time observing and cataloging natural phenomena. A bog neat the summit, and a rocky lookout off the Cliff Walk are named after him, another lookout is named after Emerson. The first recorded ascent of Mount Monadnock took place in1725 by Captain Samuel Willard and fourteen rangers under his command who camped at the top and used the summit as a lookout while patrolling for Native Americans. Monadnock is climbed by roughly 125,000 hikers yearly.

WALPOLE

ALL ABOUT WALPOLE

Walpole is a town in Cheshire County, with a current population of 3,633 (2020), and an area of 36.7 square miles. It was granted in 1726 by colonial Governor Jonathan Belcher of Massachusetts as" Number 3", third in a line of Connecticut River fort towns. It was settled in 1736 and called "Great Falls" or "Lunenberg". After the border between New Hampshire and Massachusetts was fixed, the town was regranted by Governor Benning Wentworth as "Bellowstown" after its founder, Colonel Benjamin Bellows. The grant was renewed in 1761, when the town was renamed Walpole in honor of Sir Robert Walpole, 1st Earl of Orford and first Prime Minister of Great Britain.

The town contains many architecturally significant old homes, including several associated with Colonel Bellows and members of his family. Walpole Academy, built in 1831 is listed on the National Register of Historic Places, and the abundant lilacs in the town inspired Louisa May Alcott to write the book, "Under the Lilacs". The bridge across the Connecticut River, an engineering feat in its day, was built in Walpole in 1785, and regarded as one of the most famous early spans in the United States.

PEOPLE OF SIGNIFICANCE - WALPOLE

Ken Burns (b. 1953) is an American Filmmaker, known for his style of using archival footage and photographs in his documentary films. In 1976, Burns, Elaine Mayes, and college classmate Roger Sherman founded a production company called Florentine Films in Walpole. Burns initially worked as a cinematographer for the BBC, Italian television, and others. Burns made the feature documentary, "Brooklyn Bridge" in 1981 which was narrated by David McCullough, earned an Academy Award nomination for Best Documentary and ran on PBS in the U.S. "The Civil War" received more than 40 major film and television awards, including two Emmy Awards, two Grammy Awards, the Producer of the Year Award, a People's Choice Award, a Peabody Award, and the $50,000 Lincoln Prize. As of 2017, Burns was living in Walpole with his second wife, Julie Deborah Brown, whom he married in 2003. Burns is an avid quilt collector, and about one-third of the quilts from his personal collection were displayed at the International Quilt Study Center & Museum at the University of Nebraska.

Franklin Hooper (b. 1851) was an American biologist, geologist, educator, and institute director. He was born in Walpole and grew up on his parents' farm. After three years as the head of the high school in Keene he was appointed professor of chemistry and geology at Adelphi College, Brooklyn, where he taught until 1889. In that year he was appointed as General Director of the Brooklyn Institute of Arts and Sciences. Hooper greatly expanded the institute's work of presenting a wide range of public lectures and concerts, quadrupling its membership.

Hooper was a member of the New York City Board of Education, a trustee for the Brooklyn Public Library, and president of the board of trustees at his Alma mater, Antioch College. He was the impetus behind the establishment of the New York State School of Agriculture on Long Island, and was instrumental in setting up the Old Rockingham Meeting House Association, for the preservation of the newly restores Vermont church, which his great-great grandfather helped to found in 1778.

Tom Veitch (b. 1941) was an American writer, known for his work in the comic book industry. Born in Walpole, Veitch attended Columbia University, and while living in New York City, published his first book, Literary Days in 1964. He was a contributor to the underground commix movement of the early 70s, and is known for initiating the Dark Horse Comics line of Star Wars comic books, with Dark Empire and Tales of the Jedi. Veitch died from Covid-19 in Bellows Falls, Vermont in 2022.

DO YOU KNOW WALPOLE?

The **Charles N. Vilas Bridge** is a 635-foot two-span concrete deck arch bridge over the Connecticut River between Bellows Falls, Vermont and North Walpole. Colonel Enoch Hale built a wooden covered toll bridge on this site in 1784, the first bridge over the Connecticut River. The toll was three cents for a man on horseback. The Vilas Bridge was built in 1930, and named after Charles Nathaniel Vilas of Alstead, New Hampshire, who donated funds for its construction.

Walpole Academy is an historic former school building in Walpole. Built in 1831, it is a fine rural example of Greek Revival and served the surrounding area as a private academy until 1853, and Walpole's public high school until 1950. The building was listed on the National Register of Historic Places in 1975 and is now a museum.

The **Stephan Rowe Bradley House** is a large Federal style mansion built in 1808 for Francis Gardner, a lawyer and state legislator. From 1817 to 1830, it was the home of Stephan Rowe Bradley, a Vermont lawyer, judge, and politician, who played a significant role in Vermont's entry into the U.S. as the fourteenth state. The house was listed on the National Register in 2005, and is still in the hands of his descendants.

Larry Burdick, widely regarded as a pioneer of fine chocolate in America, established in 1997 the Chocolate Shop & Café in Walpole. Now known as L.A. Burdick Handmade Chocolates, it is a purveyor of chocolates crafted by hand, artisan pastries, and gourmet drinks. For more than three decades, they have been devoted to making chocolate the time honored way-by hand.

For almost 18 years, Ken Burns, filmmaker, has been part owner of the **Restaurant at Burdick's,** a cozy nook serving French and American fare in Walpole.

JAFFREY

ALL ABOUT JAFFREY

Located along the Contoocook River, Jaffrey was first granted by the Massachusetts General Court in 1736 to soldiers returning from war in Canada. Settled in about 1758, the town was regranted in 1767, and incorporated in 1773 by Governor John Wentworth, named for George Jaffrey, a member of a wealthy Portsmouth family. With a total land area of 40.2 square miles, the main village in town where 3,058 (2020) people reside is known for its fine, early architecture including the Town Meetinghouse. Beginning in the 1840s, the area's scenic beauty attracted tourists, and several hotels were built at the base of Mount Monadnock. Jaffrey was the setting for a 1950 biography by Elizabeth Yates entitled "Amos Fortune, Free Man", winner of the 1953 Newbery Medal. Amos Fortune was an African-born slave who purchased his freedom and that of his wife, and established a tannery in the village. He is buried in the local cemetery, as is summer resident Willa Cather.

PEOPLE OF SIGNIFICANCE - JAFFREY

Laban Ainsworth (b. 1757) was an American clergyman and pastor. He holds the record for the longest serving pastorate in American history. He served as pastor in Jaffrey from 1782 to 1858, a period of 76 years, until his death at the age of 100. Suffering a severe attack of scarlet fever in childhood, Ainsworth's right arm became withered and almost useless, and as a result he was able to focus on his education. He hoped to enter Harvard in 1775, but the American Revolutionary War prevented him, and caused him instead to attend Dartmouth College, from which he graduated in 1778.

Willa Cather (b. 1873) was an American author who won a Pulitzer Prize for her World War I based novel, One of Ours, in 1923. By the 1920s, Cather was a firmly established writer, but also the subject of much criticism. By the 1930s, and increasingly large share of critics began to dismiss her as overly romantic and nostalgic, unable to grapple with contemporary issues. Despite the criticism, in 1944 Cather received the gold medal for fiction from the National Institute of Arts and Letters, a prestigious award given for an author's total accomplishments. Cather was diagnosed with breast cancer in December of 1945, and by 1947 it had metastasized to her liver becoming stage IV cancer. She died in 1947 at the age of 73, and is buried alongside her longtime partner, Edith Lewis, at the Old Burying Ground in Jaffrey.

Walter Selwyn Crosley (b. 1871) was an officer in the U.S. Navy and recipient of the Navy Cross, the second highest military decoration for valor. Born in East Jaffrey, Crosley was the son of a Universalist Church pastor. He entered the U.S. Naval academy in 1889 and graduated in 1893, then served on the USS Detroit, which was at Rio de Janeiro, Brazil, during the naval revolt against the Brazilian Government. On April 1898, he assumed his first sea-command, the USS Algonquin, and a month later was transferred to command of the American Civil War era armed tug, USS Leyden. He received the Navy Cross in 1920 for his diplomatic service in World War I, and retired in 1935 as Rear Admiral Crosley. After retirement he was elected president and director of the International Hydrographic Bureau, and served until his resignation in 1938. He died in 1939, and is buried at Arlington National

Cemetery. Admiral Crosley was a member of the Sons of the American Revolution.

Amos Fortune (b. 1710) was a prominent citizen of Jaffrey in the 18th century. He was brought to America as a slave, but purchased his freedom at the age of 60 and moved to Jaffrey to start a tannery. In 1789, Fortune purchased 25 acres on Tyler Brook, and the house and barn he built are still standing in their original location. The road the house is on is now called Amos Fortune Road. Fortune's tannery appears to have prospered. He took on at least two apprentices and served clients in Massachusetts in addition to nearby towns in New Hampshire. Fortune died in 1801 at the age of 91, and is buried behind the Jaffrey Meetinghouse in the Old Burying Ground. His wife died one year later, and was buried next to him.

DO YOU KNOW JAFFREY?

Thorndike Pond is a 252-acre body of water, 1.5 miles in length, and 0.5 miles wide, located in the towns of Dublin and Jaffrey. Located at the base of Mount Monadnock, the pond is classified as a warm water fishery, with species including smallmouth and largemouth bass, chain pickerel, horned pout, and bluegill. Whittemore Island is centrally located on the lake and contains a looping walking trail maintained by The Nature Conservatory.

The **Jaffrey Public Library** on Main Street was designed in the Romanesque Style and dedicated in 1896. It was originally named for its benefactress Susan B. Clay. The Soldiers' Monument in the front of the library was dedicated in 1900, and commemorates those who served in the American Revolution, War of 1812, and Mexican and Civil Wars.

The **Jaffrey Historic District** is the traditional heart of the town. The district lies to the west of Jaffrey's main business district, and includes the town's oldest civic buildings. The district was placed on the National Register of Historic Places in 1975. The district retains the feel of an 18th-19th century village, and includes the Old Burying Ground (1774), the Old Meetinghouse (1775), and the remnants of a tannery established in 1810. The Melville Academy, a secondary school founded in 1832, and its 1833 building is now a local museum.

COOS COUNTY

Coos County is the only New Hampshire County on the Canada-United States Border, and is home to New Hampshire's only international port of entry. Coos is the least populated county in the state, with a population of 31,268 in 2020. The only city in Coos County is Berlin, with the rest of the communities being towns or unincorporated townships. Over half of the municipal-like entities are unincorporated townships, gores, or grants, a rarity in New Hampshire, where nearly all of the land is incorporated as towns of cities.

Coos County was separated from the northern part of Grafton County in 1803. During the Revolutionary War, two units of troops were raised from the settlers of Coos: Bedel's Regiment and Whitcomb's Rangers. In the 1810 census, there were 3,991 residents, and by 1870 there were nearly 15,000 with forestry, farming and manufacturing being the major industries.

Much of its 1,830 square mile area is mountainous and reserved as national forest, wilderness, state parks, and other public areas including the northern portion of the White Mountains including all the named summits of the Presidential Range.

BERLIN

ALL ABOUT BERLIN

Berlin is the northernmost city in New Hampshire and includes the village of Cascade in the south part of the city. It's located in New Hampshire's Great North Woods Region or "North Country", sitting at the edge of the White Mountains with some of its boundaries extending into the White Mountain National Forest. Its population as of 2020 was 9,425, and has a total area of 62.2 square miles with its highest point being Mount Weeks, at 3,901 feet above sea level.

Around 11,000 years ago, small groups of Native Americans camped around what is now called Berlin. When English colonists came to America, Berlin was first granted in 1771 as "Maynesborough" after Sir William Mayne. But the grantees did not take up their claims, which disappeared with the Revolution. Maynesborough was finally settled in 1823-24 by William Sessions and his nephew Cyrus Wheeler.

With 65 inhabitants in 1829, it was finally incorporated as Berlin, and developed into a center for logging and wood industries. By 1885, the mill town was home to several pulp and paper mills that drew a number of immigrants from Russia, Norway, Finland, Sweden, Ireland, and French Canadians from nearby Quebec.

In 1872, a group of Scandinavians founded the nation's oldest ski club, which still exists today. Recent economic development has been based on the correctional industry. In 1999, the 750-bed Northern New Hampshire Correctional Facility was built, which employs approximately 200 people, and in 2012, the Federal Bureau of Prisons opened a federal, 1200-bed medium security facility, which employs approximately 350 people.

PEOPLE OF SIGNIFICANCE — BERLIN

William E. Corbin (b. 1869) moved to Berlin in 1892 where he was employed at the Riverside Mill of the Brown Company, becoming superintendent in 1894. In 1919, Corbin started to experiment to improve the problems in papermaking and completed the first paper towels in 1922. Before this there were only cloth towels - no official paper towels. This paper towel was called "Nibroc," which was Corbin spelled backwards. In October 1951, Corbin, "the father of paper towels," died at his home and was buried at Forest Hill Cemetery in Berlin. Nibroc paper towels were produced until the 1970s.

Earl Silas Tupper (b. 1907) was an American businessman and inventor, best known as the inventor of Tupperware, an airtight plastic container for storing food. Tupper founded the Tupperware Plastics Company in 1938, and in 1948 introduced Tupperware Plastics to hardware and department stores. Tupperware was withdrawn from sale in retail stores in the early 1950s, and Tupperware "parties" soon became popular in homes. This was the first instance of what became known as "party plan" marketing.

Michael Durant (b. 1961) was born in Berlin, and is an American businessman, former pilot, author, and political candidate. He was involved in the "Black Hawk Down" incident while serving as a U.S. Army pilot. He was a member of the 160th Special Operations Aviation Regiment (Night Stalkers) as a chief Warrant Officer 3. Durant published a book detailing his experiences after his retirement in 2001.

John Ramsey (b.1927), a native of Berlin, was a public address announcer best known as the original voice for the California Angels, Los Angeles Dodgers, Los Angeles Kings, Los Angeles Lakers, and Los Angeles Raiders. He was also the voice of the Los Angeles Rams and USC Trojans football and basketball teams. He also served as the basketball voice during the 1984 Summer Olympics, seven World Series, ten NBA Finals, and the 1972 NBA All-Star Games. He was noted for his articulate, deliberate, and unruffled announcing style.

Lowell Reed (b.1886) was the 7th president of John Hopkins University. Born in Berlin, he was the son of Jason Reed, a millwright and farmer. Reed had a long career as a research scientist in biostatistics and public health administration at Hopkins where he was previously dean and director of the School of Public Health. He retired in 1956, and returned to his New Hampshire farm, enjoying an active retirement until his death in 1966. Reed Hall, a residence for medical students on the Johns Hopkins medical campus, was named in his honor in 1962.

Do You Know Berlin?

Twenty-two miles northwest from Berlin, in the small town of **Stark**, is **Camp Stark**, New Hampshire's only WWII POW camp that housed German POWs from 1944-1946. At times, the population of the camp was as high as three hundred, and by all accounts the prisoners, guards, and townspeople got along surprisingly well. Paper mills were experiencing labor shortages, and German POWs fit the bill. They were paid 80 cents a day for their labor.

Jerico Mountain State Park in Berlin is a 7,493-acre State Park containing 50-60 miles of ATV trails, the only major state-owned ATV riding area in New Hampshire. The park also has a 4x4 Jeep and truck trail, the first one on public land in the northeastern United States. The park's namesake, 2,454-foot Jerico Mountain, is located just outside the park to the east. **Mount Jasper Lithic Source** is a prehistoric archaeo-logical site in Berlin, and includes one of the only known evidences of mining by pre-Contact Native Americans in the eastern U.S. Evidence from this site indicates it was a source of stone for tools as much as 9,000 years ago.

CAN YOU IDENTIFY THIS PHOTO? The Holy Resurrection Orthodox Church was built in 1915 by immigrants from the Russian Empire. In 1915, Reverend Arcady Piotrowski came to Berlin to establish an Orthodox church for the approximately 500 Russians that inhabited Berlin at that time.

DIXVILLE NOTCH

ALL ABOUT DIXVILLE NOTCH

Dixville Notch is an unincorporated community in Coos County with a population of four, as of the 2020 census. It is located in the northern part of the state, approximately 20 miles south of the Canadian province of Quebec, and situated at about 1,800 feet above sea level.

The village is known for being one of the first places to declare its results during United States presidential elections and the New Hampshire presidential primary. Dixville Notch was granted the authority to conduct its own elections in 1960 and chose to open its polls at midnight. Since then, Dixville Notch has gained international media attention as the first community to vote in the presidential primary season, and also votes at midnight in the general presidential election in November. In 2019, the community was at risk of losing its ability to conduct its own election and having to combine with another municipality, as its population had been reduced to four people - one too few to hold all the positions needed to conduct an election in New Hampshire. Dixville Notch received a reprieve, however, when a fifth person (Les Otten, developer of the Balsams) agreed to move there in time for the election.

The village shares its name with Dixville Notch, a mountain pass that lies about 0.5 miles from the town itself, and is the home of the Balsams Grand Resort Hotel, one of a handful of surviving New Hampshire grand hotels.

PEOPLE OF SIGNIFICANCE – DIXVILLE NOTCH

Neil Tillotson (b.1898) was the inventor of the modern production of methods for latex balloons and latex gloves, and the founder of Tillotson Rubber Company. As a resident of Dixville Notch, he was the first voter in every American presidential primary and presidential election for forty years, until his death at age 102. In 1954 Tillotson purchased The Balsams Grand Hotel in Dixville Notch where the first in the nation primary is held.

Do You Know Dixville Notch?

The Balsams Grand Resort Hotel first opened after the Civil War as the Dix House, a 25-room summer inn. In 1895, it was purchased by Henry S. Hale who had been a regular guest; he renamed it "The Balsams". Hale enlarged the facilities, expanding the resort's capacity to 400 guests. The Ballot Room of the Balsams is where Dixville Notch's presidential primary votes are cast after midnight on the day of the NH primary. Resort grounds cover 11,000 acres, and feature 59 miles of cross-country ski trails, an alpine ski area with 16 trails, five glade areas and a terrain park. There is a nine-hole golf course and an 18-hole championship course called "Panorama", designed by Donald Ross.

STARK

All About Stark

Stark is a town in Coos County, originally granted in 1774 and named "Percy", after Hugh Percy, 1st Duke of Northumberland. The town was incorporated in 1832 and renamed "Stark" after General John Stark who wrote the words that became New Hampshire's motto, "Live Free or Die". Much of the town's 59.7 square miles are within the boundaries of the White Mountain National Forest, including several peaks higher than 3,000 feet, in 2020 had a population of 478.

People of Significance – Stark

General John Stark was born in Londonderry (at a site now in Derry) in 1728, and the original town of "Percy" was renamed "Stark" in 1832, in his honor. Stark survived capture by the Abenaki Indians, served with the famous Rogers Rangers in the French and Indian War, fought at Bunker Hill, the battles of Princeton and Trenton and contributed to the surrender of Burgoyne's northern army at the battle of Saratoga. He sat as a judge in the court martial of John Andre, guilty of spying and helping in the conspiracy of Benedict Arnold to surrender West Point to the British. He was commander of the Northern Department three times between 1778-1781, along with commanding a brigade at the Battle of Springfield in 1780. He retired to his farm in Derryfield, renamed Manchester in 1810, dying in 1882 at the age of 93.

Do You Know Stark?

Stark Covered Bridge is an historic wooden covered bridge over the Upper Ammonoosuc River in Stark, listed on the National Register of Historic Places in 1980. At 151 feet long and twenty-nine feet wide, it was built in either 1857 or 1862 to replace a floating bridge. The bridge is reinforced with steel beams, with a carrying capacity of 15 tons. It is decorated with pendant acorn finials and painted bright white.

Camp Stark was a converted Civilian Conservation Corps camp, which held about 250 German POWs. It was the only World War II POW camp in NH, with most of the men in camp working in the nearby forests supplying wood for the paper mills. Some of the men eventually came back to live in the U.S. after the war. The camp was closed in 1946.

PITTSBURG

All About Pittsburg

Pittsburg is the northernmost town in New Hampshire, and the largest town by area in New England, most of it undeveloped. Its population in 2020 was 800, and it derives its name from William Pitt, Prime Minister of Great Britain. Prior to its incorporation in 1840, the area was settled around 1810 and known as the Territory of Indian Stream. It had the unique distinction of having been its own microstate briefly during the 1830s, called the Republic of Indian Stream, due to an ambiguous boundary between the United States and Canada.

Pittsburg is the only New Hampshire municipality to border Canada, and the only one that borders both Maine and Vermont. It has a total area of 291.3 square miles, making it the largest in New Hampshire and New England of any municipality incorporated as a town. The highest point in Pittsburg is the summit of Stub Hill, at 3,627 feet.

People of Significance

Luther Parker (b. 1800) was an American pioneer, teacher, and politician, who served as justice of the peace of the Republic of Indian Stream, located in what is now Pittsburg. Parker and his wife moved to what would become the Republic of Indian Stream, where he operated a store, and helped draft the Indian Stream Constitution, a role that made him one of the primary leaders of the Republic. In Pittsburg there is a marker on the shore of First Connecticut Lake commemorating Parker's contributions to the Republic of Indian Stream.

DO YOU KNOW PITTSBURG?

Pittsburg is a destination for snowmobile and ATV enthusiasts year-round. During the winter months, thousands of people take advantage of the state-funded and club-supported and maintained trails with access to the states of Maine, Vermont, and the border crossing to Canada. Another focus in the area for tourists is fishing and hunting. Pittsburg is home to the four Connecticut lakes, Back Lake, part of Lake Francis, and numerous smaller bodies of water. The area is known for fly-fishing, and has attracted anglers since the early 1900s.

Lake Francis State Park is a public recreation area located on Lake Francis in Pittsburg. It covers 17 acres of land on Lake Francis, and offers a boat launch, visitor center, playground, and camping.

Deer Mountain Camp Ground is located on **Connecticut Lake State** Forest in Pittsburg, and covers roughly 1,648 acres, just five minutes from the Canadian border. There are 25 primitive sites, and the area is known for moose watching.

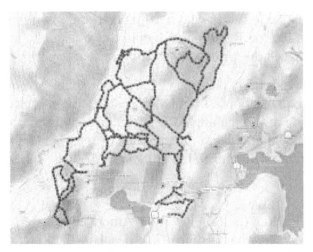

CAN YOU IDENTIFY THIS IMAGE? Map of ATV/UTV Riding Trails in Pittsburg

GORHAM

ALL ABOUT GORHAM

Gorham is a town in Coos County first chartered in 1770 by colonial governor John Wentworth as a part of Shelburne, called "Shelburne Addition". It was first settled about 1802, but for years contained little more than rocky farms and small logging operations. When incorporated in 1836, the town had only 150 inhabitants. It was named "Gorham" at the suggestion of a resident from Gorham, Maine, and a relative of the Gorham family who incorporated the town in 1764.

Gorham is located in the White Mountains, and parts of the **White Mountain National Forest**, and has a population of 1,851 as of the 2020 census. It has a total area of 32.3 square miles, and when the railroad arrived in 1851, Gorham developed into a railroad town. Railroads ben-efitted local industries as well, hauling freight for mills run by water power from the Androscoggin River. In 1861, travelers made the first trek up the Mount Washington Carriage Road, winding eight miles to the summit of the 6,388-foot mountain. "The Road to the Sky" was an engi-neering feat of its day, advertised as "the first man-made attraction in the United States". It would later be renamed the **Mount Washington Auto Road**, which is still popular today. Business would eventually decline, as did the railroads. In 1973, the town's train depot, built in 1907, was scheduled for demolition. The Gorham Historical Society saved the building, which now serves as a museum.

PEOPLE OF SIGNIFICANCE – GORHAM

Albert Johnson (d.1988) was a doctor who, along with his family, passed as white in Gorham and Keene, New Hampshire. He was from Chicago, interned at Maine General Hospital, but had trouble finding work, eventually securing employment as a doctor by passing for white. He was a country doctor and radiologist in Gorham and Keene. He en-tered the Navy as a commissioned officer, but the offer was rescinded as a result of his ethnic background. His experiences were adapted to both film and book.

Do You Know Gorham?

Moose Brook State Park was constructed during the Great Depression by workers from the Civilian Conservation Corps. The park occupies 755 acres, and sits at an elevation of 1.070 feet. The corps built park facilities and trails using the natural resources at hand. Cabins and other facilities were built with rocks and logs taken from the land surrounding their construction site. The original park offices are still in use today.

The park lies within the White Mountains, which are a part of the larger Appalachian Mountains, and is named for Moose Brook, a tributary of the Androscoggin River. There are 59 campsites at the park in a variety of areas, and is often used as a base for visitors to the White Mountains and the **Presidential Range**.

CAN YOU IDENTIFY THIS PHOTO? Nansen Ski Jump, also known as The Big Nansen and The Sleeping Giant, is a ski jump located along Route 16 in Milan, in Coos County. Built in 1936, it was the largest ski jump of its time and now has been restored. It is now within the Nansen Ski Jump State Historic Site, a New Hampshire state park. Named for Norwegian explorer and humanitarian Fridtjof Nansen, the ski jump has been listed on the National Register of Historic Places.

GRAFTON COUNTY

Grafton County is a county in the northwest part of New Hampshire. As of the 2020 census, the population was 91,118 covering an area of 1,749.7 square miles. Grafton was one of the five counties originally identified for New Hampshire in 1769, and named for Augustus FitzRoy, 3rd Duke of Grafton who had been a supporter of American causes in Parliament, and who was serving as British Prime Minister at the time. The county was organized at Woodsville in 1771, and originally included the entire northern frontier of New Hampshire. In 1797, the county had 50 townships, 17 locations, and a population of 12,093.

Grafton County is heavily rural, with about half of its area in the White Mountain National Forest. Many of the 4,000-foot mountains of New Hampshire are located within the county, and the Appalachian Trail passes through parts of at least ten towns in the county.

HANOVER

ALL ABOUT HANOVER

Hanover, located along the Connecticut River in Grafton County, is the home of Dartmouth College, and the U.S. Army Corps of Engineers Cold Regions Research and Engineering laboratory. The Appalachian Trail crosses the town, connecting with a number of trails and nature preserves.

Hanover was chartered by Governor Benning Wentworth in 1761, with its first European inhabitants arriving a few years later. The town developed into an agricultural community. Dartmouth College was established in 1769 beside the town common called "the Plain"- an extensive and level tract of land a mile from the Connecticut River. The town has a total area of 50.2 square miles, and a population of 11,870 (2020). The highest point is the north peak of Moose Mountain, at 2,313 feet. CNN and Money Magazine rated Hanover as the sixth best place to live in America in 2011, and the second best in 2007.

PEOPLE OF SIGNIFICANCE – HANOVER

Richard Ghormley Eberhart (b. 1904) was a Pulitzer Prize winning poet, who published more than a dozen books of poetry, and approximately twenty books in total. He died in Hanover in 2005 at age 101, after teaching for thirty years at Dartmouth as professor of English and poet–in–residence, where he was known for encouraging young poets. President Dwight Eisenhower appointed him a member of the Advisory Committee on the Arts for the National Cultural Center in 1959, and he was Poet Laureate Consultant in Poetry to the Library of Congress for 1959-1961. He was awarded the Bollingen Prize in 1962.

William McGuire Bryson (b.1951) is an American-British author of nonfiction books on topics including travel, the English language, and science. From 1995 to 2003, Bryson lived in Hanover, during which time he published *Notes from a Small Island,* which was also made into a television series, and *A Short History of Nearly Everything,* a book widely acclaimed for its accessible communication of science. Bryson has been awarded many honorary doctorates, and currently lives in rural New Hampshire, while maintaining a small flat in Kensington, London.

Jodi Picoult (b.1966) is an American writer who has published 27 novels, with approximately 40 million copies of her books in print world-wide. Picoult has been married to Timothy Warren van Leer since 1989, and they reside in Hanover with their three children. *Nineteen Minutes* was her first book to debut at number one on the New York Times best-seller list, and *Change of Heart*, published a year later, was her second novel to debut at number one on that list. Picoult has won many honors and awards over her career, and in 2017, she spoke at the New Hampshire Women's Day of Action and Unity in support of the Women's March on Washington.

Hal Barwood (b. 1940) is an American film producer, director, game designer, and novelist. He was born in Hanover, where his father ran a local movie theater, which inspired him to become involved in the film industry. His first film work was when he worked as animator in George Lucas' first theatrical film, "THX 1138", later to become a cult classic, and later worked on the script of "Close Encounters of the Third Kind", eventually grossing over $337 million worldwide. Following his departure from LucasArts in2003, Barwood founded his own video game company named Finite Arts.

C. Everett Koop (b. 1916) was an American pediatric surgeon, and public health administrator, who served as the 13th Surgeon General of the United States under President Ronald Reagan from 1982-1989. He has won numerous awards and honors, including a number of publications. Koop died February 25, 2103, at the age of 96 at his home in Hanover, New Hampshire.

Thomas Kinkaid (b. 1888) was an admiral in the United States Navy, known for his service during WWII. Born in Hanover, New Hampshire Kinkaid was the second child and only son of Thomas Wright Kinkaid, a naval officer. In November 1943, Kinkaid became Commander Allied Forces South West Pacific Area, and Commander of the Seventh Fleet, where he commanded allied ships in the last naval battle between battleships in history. The Navy named a Spruance-class destroyer after him. USS Kinkaid was launched on June1, 1974. He was buried with full military honors at Arlington National Cemetery.

Do You Know Hanover?

Dartmouth College, established in 1769, is one of nine colleges chartered before the American Revolution. Founded to educate Native Americans in Christian Theology and the English way of life, the university-trained Congregationalist ministers during its early history. Located in Hanover, it is situated on a terrace above the Connecticut River. Dartmouth's main campus is in the rural Upper Valley region of New England. As a liberal arts institution, Dartmouth has 39 academic departments offering 56 major programs, and its Economics Department holds the distinction as the top-ranked bachelors-only economics program in the world. Dartmouth boasts a number of distinguished alumni. In 1972, Dartmouth College became coeducational.

The **Hood Museum of Art** located in Hanover is owned and operated by Dartmouth College. The first reference to the development of an art collection at Dartmouth dates to 1772, making the collection among the oldest and largest of any college or university museum in the country. The Hood Museum's collection of 65,000 objects represents the diverse artistic traditions of six continents.

The **Dartmouth Skiway** boasts a much-decorated racing history, with prominent ski team alumni. Dartmouth College was "the collegiate champion of the outdoor life and winter sports" in the early 1900s, and a number of men skied for the United States in the 1936 Winter Olympics in Germany. The Dartmouth Skiway has a long, colorful role in American ski history.

LITTLETON

All About Littleton

Situated at the northern edge of the White Mountains, Littleton has a population of 6,005 in 2020, and a total area of fifty-four square miles bounded on the northwest by the Connecticut River. Originally called "Chiswick" (Saxon for "Cheese Farm") in 1764, the area was settled in 1769. Later on, the land was passed to Colonel Moses Little, a Surveyor of the King's woods, and the town was named in his honor when it was incorporated in1784, the same year New Hampshire became a state.

The Connecticut River serves as the state boundary with Vermont, and its highest point is the summit of Towns Mountain at 2,203 feet. Located on the banks of the Ammonoosuc River is the Littleton Grist Mill, first opened in 1798, which has been restored to its original appearance. Between 1867 and 1909, the local Kilburn Brothers factory published photographs and stereoviews, ands old stereoscopes, double-picture viewers popular in the Victorian age.

PEOPLE OF SIGNIFICANCE - LITTLETON

Richard Blackwell Gale (b. 1954) is a former starting pitcher in Major League Baseball. Born in Littleton, Gale went to the University of New Hampshire on a basketball scholarship, but made his mark on the baseball diamond. Selected by the Kansas City Royals in 1975, he entered the Majors in 1978 with the Royals, playing four years with them before joining the San Francisco Giants (1982), Cincinnati Reds (1983), and the Boston Red Sox (1984).

Dorothy Ann Eckels Bailie (b. 1935) is an American mathematician who worked at the Goddard Space Flight Center, one of three authors of the 1959 report establishing Earth's shape as asymmetrical, based on data from Vanguard 1. Born in Littleton, she earned a bachelor's degree in mathematics from Middlebury College in 1957. After college, she worked at the U.S. Naval Research Laboratory, and by 1959 she worked at the Theoretical Division of NASA'S Goddard Space Flight Center, calculating complex orbits for satellites. She has authored a number of publications and reports, and later in her career she worked at Analytical Mechanics Associates in Maryland.

Hugh Galen (b. 1924) was an American automobile dealer and Democratic politician from Littleton. Galen served as the 74th governor of New Hampshire from 1979 until his death in 1982.

Eleanor H. Porter (b. 1868) was an American novelist, best known for *Pollyanna* (1913). Born in Littleton, she was trained as a singer, attending the New England Conservatory for several years. Porter achieved considerable commercial success, as *Pollyanna* ranked eighth among best-selling novels in the United States during 1913, and with 47 printings between 1915 and 1920. Although Porter wrote mainly children's literature, she also wrote more adult novels and short stories.

Do You Know Littleton?

Littleton Coin Company is an employee-owned privately held major American mail order and retail company focused on numismatic collectibles. It focuses largely on U.S. coins, world coins, and a variety of paper money and ancient coins. Largely focused on direct mail, the Littleton Con Company publishes catalogs several times yearly.

Chutters Candy Store, with its New England style brick architecture, located on Main Street, boasts its 112 feet of the original Guinness World Record candy counter. The **Pollyanna Statue** is the centerpiece of downtown Littleton, and tribute to hometown author Eleanor Porter. **Wallace Horse Cemetery** is a plot of fenced in land where Eli Wallace had three horses buried. Maud and Molly in 1919, and Maggie in 1929, were buried with "all of their trappings".

PLYMOUTH

All About Plymouth

Located at the confluence of the Pemigewasset and Baker Rivers, Plymouth is a rural town in Grafton County that sits at the foot of the White Mountains, with a total area of 28.6 square miles. With a population of 6,682 at the 2020 census, Plymouth is home to Plymouth State University, which has an undergraduate class size of 4,000 students, and a graduate class size of 1,000 students.

Plymouth was originally the site of an Abenaki village burned to the ground by Captain Thomas Baker in 1712, one of the many British raids on American Indian settlements during Queen Anne's War. The town was first named "New Plymouth", after the original Plymouth Colony in Massachusetts. The town was incorporated in 1763.

In 1806, then-lawyer Daniel Webster lost his first criminal case at Plymouth Courthouse, which now houses the Historical Society, and in 1864, while on vacation with former U.S. President Franklin Pierce, author Nathaniel Hawthorne died at the second Pemigewasset House, which was later destroyed by fire in 1909. The Plymouth Normal School was founded in 1871, becoming the state's first teacher's college.

PEOPLE OF SIGNIFICANCE - PLYMOUTH

Eliza Coupe (b. 1981) is an American actress, comedian, and model. Born and raised in Plymouth, she is best known for her roles in the ABC comedy series, *Happy Endings,* and in the final two seasons of the medical comedy-drama, *Scrubs.* In 2005, her one-woman sketch shows *The Patriots,* premiered in New York, and won her the Breakout Performer Award at HBO's U.S. Comedy Arts Festival in Aspen, Colorado, in March 2006. In April 2020, she was cast as Amy in the Fox comedy series *Pivoting,* debuting in 2022 with positive reviews.

Harl Pease (b. 1917) was a U.S. Army Air Corps officer and recipient of The Medal of Honor for his actions during World War II. He was the namesake for Pease Air Force Base, now Pease Air National Guard Base. Pease was born and raised in Plymouth, attending the University of New Hampshire where he graduated in 1939.

In August, 1942, one engine of Pease's B-17 failed during a mission, forcing it to return to base. With only three hours of rest, the crew took off again. While 40-50 miles from the target, the group was attacked by more than 30 Japanese fighters. Pease and his crew fought their way through to the target, and bombed successfully, but sustained heavy damage. As he fell behind, he was attacked again, but before the B-17 crashed Pease and another crew member were able to bail out. Both men were captured and sent to a POW camp in Rabul. The remains of Pease's crew were found and identified, though the remains of Pease were not recovered. The Medal of Honor was awarded posthumously to Pease.

William F. Batchelder (b. 1926) was a justice of the NH Supreme Court from 1981-1995. He graduated from Plymouth Regional High School in 1944, and enlisted in the U.S. Navy during World War II. After the war, Batchelder received a Bachelor's degree from the University of New Hampshire, and a law degree from Boston University School of Law. He was later appointed to the New Hampshire Superior Court in 1970, and to the state supreme court in 1981. The William F. Batchelder Justice Fund, established by the New Hampshire Bar Association, supports legal assistance for low income and disadvantaged people. He died peacefully at his home in Plymouth on January 25, 1987.

Do You Know Plymouth?

Fox Park Trails – New England Mountain Bike Association has several long, hand built, long looping switchbacking trails, with quite a few hills to climb. There are plenty of light, tight technical sections, and lots of hand-made berms on the lighter corners, followed by some smooth downhills. The trails are rated moderate to difficult.

Museum of the White Mountains provides access to resources and activities that educate its audience with the region's artistic, historical, geographic, and cultural treasures.

The Flying Monkey is a vintage movie house from the 1920s featuring a variety of events, plus dining and beverage service. It opened as the "New Plymouth Theater" in the 1920s, as a vaudeville and silent film theater. After falling into disrepair, it was bought, renovated, and opened as the Flying Monkey Movie House & Performance Center.

Tenney Mountain, a ski and snowboard area in Plymouth, offers 45 trails over 110 acres of skiable terrain. The ski area has a summit elevation of 2,149 feet with the majority of trails at intermediate to expert levels. The resort has been in operation for around 50 years.

The **Pemigewasset House** was named for the river that runs behind it. The hotel is probably best known as the place where Nathaniel Hawthorne died. In the spring of 1864, Hawthorne, who had been in poor health, took a trip to recuperate. He and travelling companion, Franklin Pierce, stayed at the hotel in May 1864. The next morning, Pierce woke to discover that Hawthorne had died in his sleep, at the age of 59.

WATERVILLE VALLEY

All About Waterville Valley

Waterville Valley was first settled in the 1760s and incorporated as "Waterville" in 1829. The name "Waterville Valley" was adopted in 1967. The town has a total area of 64.4 square miles, and a population of 508 at the 2020 census. The highest point in Waterville Valley is the North Peak of Mount Tripyramid, at 4,180 feet. Other 4,000-footers in the town include Mount Tecumseh listed at 4,003 feet, and mounts

Whiteface at 4,019 feet, and Passaconaway at 4.043 feet. Sandwich Mountain, at 3,983 feet is on the southern border.

The Waterville Valley Elementary School is also known as the "Little Red School." Students are able to swim, bike, ski, skate, and play tennis in Waterville Valley. The Waterville Valley Academy is a ski academy founded in 1972, with the campus located at the foot of Snow's Mountain. It is part of the WVBBTS ski club.

PEOPLE OF SIGNIFICANCE – WATERVILLE VALLEY

Thomas Corcoran (b. 1931) was a four-time U.S. national champion in alpine skiing, and two-time Olympian. In addition to seven years of international ski racing, Corcoran raced for Dartmouth College. After his racing career, he opened the Waterville Valley Resort, serving as an executive until 1990. He was inducted into the National Ski Hall of Fame in 1978 and presented with the first New England Ski Museum Spirit of Skiing Award in 2006. He died June 27, 2017, at the age of 85.

John E. Sununu (b. 1939) served as a member of the U.S. House of Representatives and as a U.S. Senator, and was the youngest member of the Senate for his entire six-year term. He was the 75th governor of New Hampshire from 1983-1989. He served as CEO and General Manager of Waterville Valley Resort.

H.A. Rey (b. 1898), a German-born American illustrator and author, co-wrote the *Curious George* books with wife **Margret Rey (b. 1906)**. Married for 42 years, they summered in Waterville Valley.

DO YOU KNOW WATERVILLE VALLEY?

Waterville Valley Resort is a European-style getaway nestled within the White Mountain National Forest, surrounded by 360 degrees of mountains. It features 265 skiable acres with an altitude of 4,004 feet, and vertical drop of 2,020 feet. Winter activities include skiing, snowboarding, cross country skiing, snowshoeing, fat bike riding, tubing, skating, sleigh riding, and dogsled excursions. Waterville Valley is the birthplace of Freestyle Skiing.

Known for its wide range of **sports activities**, organized skiing first started on **Mount Tecumseh** in the 1930s with the construction of two

Civilian Conservation Corps ski trails. **Waterville Valley Skate Camp** is the only overnight camp in New England run by skateboarders, and overnight campers stay in the heart of Town Square, steps away from the State Park, restaurants and shops. **Waterville Valley Ice Arena**, located adjacent to the Town Square on Corcoran Pond, offers public skating sessions and is home to the Hockey Academy, hosting many youth hockey tournaments. **Waterville Valley's historic golf course** opened in 1898 and underwent a major renovation in 2005.

WOODSVILLE

Woodsville is the largest village in Haverhill, along the Connecticut River at the mouth of the Ammonoosuc River, with a population of 1,431. Although North Haverhill is now the county seat, the village of Woodsville was traditionally considered the county seat, as the county courthouse was originally located there. In *The Stand* by Stephen King, Woodsville is mentioned as the home of Glen Pequod Bateman, a major character in the novel. He was an associate professor of sociology at the fictional Woodsville Community College when the superflu hit.

Ann Stone Minot (April 25, 1894 – 1980) was an American bio-chemist and physiologist. She was born in Woodsville, the oldest of six children born to Jonas Minot and Sybil Buck. Minot and her siblings attended the Bath Village School, a three-room schoolhouse. Minot matriculated to Smith College with a partial scholarship, and majored in chemistry and English. She graduated in 1915 with an A.B. degree. Her first full-time job was as a teacher at Woodsville High School.

Bob Smith and Chad Paronto of Woodsville (population 1100) are former major league baseball pitchers. Both pitched for multiple major league teams. Bob Smith pitched for the Red Sox in one game. **T. Borden Walker** known as the "King of the Valley" owned a furniture and appliance store on the Dartmouth College Highway. A former State leader of the Lions Club and Republican Party State Chairman, he was the main force behind the fundraising and building of the Cottage Hospital.

HILLSBOROUGH COUNTY

Hillsborough was one of the five original counties identified for New Hampshire in 1769, and was named for Wills Hill, 1st Earl of Hillsborough, who was British Secretary of State for the colonies at the time. The county was formally organized at Amherst in 1771. Hillsborough County's administrative functions were moved from Amherst to Milford in 1866, and then to the current seats of Manchester and Nashua in 1869.

The county has a total area of 892 square miles, with the highest point being Pack Monadnock Mountain at 2,290 feet. Hillsborough County is the most populous county in the state with a population of 422,937 as of the 2020 census, almost one-third the population of the entire state. It is also the most densely populated county at 482.8 inhabitants per square mile with its two biggest cities of Manchester and Nashua.

MANCHESTER

ALL ABOUT MANCHESTER

Manchester is the most populous city in northern New England. At 34 square miles, and a population of 116,644, it was first named by inventor Samuel Blodgett whose vision was to create a great industrial center similar to that of the original Manchester in England. The native Pennacook people called Amoskeag Falls on the Merrimack River the area that became the heart of Manchester-'Namoskeag', meaning good fishing place.

In 1772, John Goffe III settled by Cohas Brook, later building a dam and sawmill. It was granted by Massachusetts in 1727 as "Tyngstown" to veterans of Queen Anne's War who served in 1703 under Captain William Tyng. But at New Hampshire's 1741 separation from Massachusetts, the grant was ruled invalid resulting in a 1751 rechartering by Governor Benning Wentworth as "Derryfield". In 1809, Benjamin Pritchard and others built a water-powered cotton spinning mill on the western bank of the Merrimack River, and "Derryfield" was renamed Manchester. In 1810 the mill was incorporated as the Amoskeag Cotton and Woolen Manufacturing Company.

Today, Manchester is the home of the Fisher Cats minor league baseball team, unique attractions, and great museums and restaurants. The Currier Museum of Art features works by major American and European artists and operates the Frank Lloyd Wright-designed Zimmerman House. In an old fabric mill, the Millyard Museum traces how the nearby Amoskeag Falls shaped the city and its textile industry, and trails in the sprawling Derryfield Park lead to the 19th century Weston Observatory. Less than an hour from the Atlantic Coast and 90 miles from the White Mountains and Lakes Region, Manchester attracts many visitors from both near and far.

PEOPLE OF SIGNIFICANCE - MANCHESTER

Adam Sandler (b. 1966) is an American comedian, actor, and filmmaker. He was a cast member on Saturday Night Live from 1990-

1995 before going on to star in many Hollywood films. Sandler moved to Manchester at the age of six, and attended Manchester Central High School, and in 2007, Sandler made a donation of $100,000 to the Boys and Girls Clubs of America in Manchester.

Robert William Montana (b. 1920) was an American comic strip artist who created the original likenesses for the characters published by Archie Comics, and in the newspaper strip Archie. He graduated from Manchester High School Central, and according to a classmate Archie and his friends were based on people from their hometown and high school. Montana was soon drawing the Archie comic strip, which over the next 35 ran in over 750 newspapers.

Grace Metalious (b. 1924) was an American author best known for her novel *Peyton Place*, one of the best-selling works in publishing history. Writing at an early age, at Manchester Central High School, she also acted in school plays. In the fall of 1954, at the age of 30 she began work on a manuscript about the dark secrets of a small New England town. Published in September of 1956, it was dismissed by most critics, yet it remained on the New York Times bestseller list for more than a year and became an international phenomenon.

Ralph Henry Baer (b. 1922) was a German-American inventor, game developer, and engineer. He was working as an engineer at Sanders Associates (now BAE Systems) when he conceived the idea of playing games on a television screen around 1966. He worked through several prototypes until he arrived at a "Brown Box" that would later become the blueprint for the first home video game console, licensed as the Magnavox Odyssey. He continued to work in electronics until his death in 2014, with over 150 patents to his name.

Do You Know Manchester?

The Currier Museum of Art was founded in 1929 by former New Hampshire governor, Moody Currier, and established "for the benefit and advancement of humanity. The museum contains artwork from Monet, Picasso, Matisse, and countless other pieces of both American and European paintings, decorative arts, photographs and sculpture.

McIntyre Ski Area is a city owned ski area adjacent to Derryfield Park. It was opened in 1971 with two chair lifts and a rope tow. It offers lessons, rentals, snowboarding, tubing, and hosts a number of races, fundraisers, and other competitions throughout the winter season.

The **Manchester Historic Association's Millyard Museum** is worth a visit. The museum is housed in Mill #3 at the corner of Commercial and Pleasant streets in the historic Amoskeag Millyard. One of the permanent exhibits, "Woven in Time" tells the story of 11,000 years at Amoskeag Falls, and the people who have lived and worked there. The story begins with the native peoples who fished at the falls 11,000 years ago and continues with displays on the area's early farmers and lumbermen, as well as the beginnings of industry in the area.

The Zimmerman and Kalil houses were the first two houses in New Hampshire designed by Frank Lloyd Wright. Built on the same street in 1951 and 1955. The Currier Museum provides tours of the buildings which is the only legal access to the grounds. The home was donated to the museum after the death of Dr. Isadore Zimmerman, and in 1979 was listed on the National Register of Historic Places.

Housed in the Manchester Airport's former terminal, the **Aviation Museum** focuses on New Hampshire's aviation history, and features exhibits showing how it served as a primary staging area for army planes heading to Europe during World War II. Originally built in 1937, this Art Deco building was moved across two active runways to its current spot where it has been fully restored.

CAN YOU IDENTIFY THIS PHOTO? The Currier Art Museum in Manchester

NASHUA

ALL ABOUT NASHUA

Nashua is a city in southern New Hampshire with a population of 89,052 (2020), covering about 31.73 miles. The Nashua River was named by the Nashaway people, and in the Pennacook language it means "beautiful stream with a pebbly bottom" with an alternative meaning of, "land between two rivers." In 1842 the town split into two towns, but eleven years later joined back together under the name "Nashua". Today, Nashua is the second largest city in Northern New England after nearby Manchester, and along with Manchester is a seat of New Hampshire's most populous county-Hillsborough.

Originally, the area was part of a 200-mile tract of land in Massachusetts called "Dunstable", named after Edward Tyng of Dunstable, England, and first settled in 1654 as a fur trading town. Later on, like many19th century river front New England communities. New Hampshire's Dunstable was developed during the Industrial Revolution with textile mills operated from water power. In 1823 the Nashua Manufacturing Company was incorporated, and eventually had four mills and employed approximately1.000 workers. The following year Manufacturing Company was incorporated. At its height, six railroads crossed the mill town, and like the rival Amoskeag Manufacturing Company upriver, the Nashua mills prospered until about World War I, after which a slow decline set in. Water power was replaced with other forms of energy such as coal, and cotton could not be manufactured into fabric where it grew, saving transportation costs. The textile business started moving to the South during the Great Depression, with the last mill near Nashua closing in 1949.

More recently, Nashua's economy to the financial services, high tech, and defense industries as a part of the economic recovery started in the 1980's. The city is now home to several major private employers including BAE and Teradyne and hosts two major medical centers: Southern New Hampshire Medical Center, and St. Joseph Hospital. Twice named by Money Magazine as the "Best Place to Live in America" (1987 and 1998), the South Nashua Commercial District is a major regional shopping destination, lying directly on the Massachusetts border and taking advantage of New Hampshire's lack of a sales tax.

PEOPLE OF SIGNIFICANCE - NASHUA

Thomas Reardon (b. 1969) is an American computational neuroscientist and the CEO and co-founder of CTRL-Labs. Formerly, he was a computer programmer and developer at Microsoft, and credited with creating the project to build Microsoft's web browser, Internet Explorer, which was the world's most used browser during its peak in the early 2000s. Following the acquisition of CTRL-Labs, he leads the neural interfaces group at Facebook Reality Labs.

Walter Huntley Long (b.1879) was an American character actor in films from the 1910's. He appeared in many D.W. Griffith films, notably "The Birth of a Nation" (1915). He supported Rudolph Valentino in the films, "The Sheik", "Moran of the Lady Letty", and "Blood and Sand", and appeared as a comic villain in four Laurel and Hardy films.

Alvin Augustus Lucier (b. 1911) was an American composer of experimental music and sound installations that explore acoustic phenomena and auditory perception. Much of his work was influenced by science and explores the physical properties of sound itself, and the transmission of sound through physical media, and was a member of the influential Sonic Arts Union.

Amanda Lee Moore (b. 1984) is an American singer, songwriter, and actress, who rose to fame with her debut single, "Candy", which peaked at number 41 on the Billboard Hot 100. Her debut studio album, "So Real" received a platinum certification from the RAIA. Moore has sold 2.7 million albums in the U.S. according to Billboard. Moore made her feature film debut in 2001, with a minor voice role in the film, "Dr. Doolittle 2, before starring as Lana Thomas in the comedy film, "The Princess Diaries". She has won two Screen Actors Guild Awards for Outstanding Performance by an Ensemble in a Drama series, and in 2019, was awarded a star on the Hollywood walk of Fame.

John G. Foster (b. 1823) was a career military officer in the U.S. Army, and a Union General during the American Civil War. He became second in command during the Battle of Fort Sumter, and later appointed to command the 1st Brigade in Major General Ambrose Burnside's North

Carolina Expedition. He was a veteran of many Civil Was battles, and at the end of the war was assigned to command the Department of Florida, receiving a promotion to the rank of major general.

Bob Boisvert (b. 1948) is the President of Masi Plumbing Heating and A/C in Nashua that is one of the top-rated plumbing and heating companies in the State of New Hampshire. Bob has served on a number of boards of non-profit institutions in Nashua.

Samuel A. Tamposi, of Nashua, who rose from modest beginnings as a farmer and vacuum cleaner salesman to become New Hampshire's largest commercial real estate developer, died in 1995. Mr. Tamposi made his fortune buying and selling land and persuading Fortune 500 companies like Anheuser-Busch, Digital Equipment and Raytheon to build plants in New Hampshire. Former Senator Warren Rudman said that Mr. Tamposi "brought more jobs to New Hampshire than all of the economic authorities in all of the state's cities and townships put together."

The Nashua Corporation's products were gummed flats, gummed paper, and sock linings, and later added glazed paper, cardboard, and "surface coated" paper. The whole city of Nashua worked at the mill in the 1930s through the 1960s.

Doehla Greeting Cards Inc. set up a new headquarters in Nashua in 1951, where the newly invested property would be "large enough to handle all of its manufacturing operations under one roof and still allow the company to expand." The move brought in women workers which hadn't previously worked at paper-producing plant. Founder **Harry Doehla** was known as a pioneer for creating a healthy and welcoming work environment.

DO YOU KNOW NASHUA?

Constructed in 1937, **Holman Stadium** is a multi-purpose stadium with an official seating capacity of 2,800 people. Named for Charles Frank Holman who contributed $55,000 for the project, it was dedicated to the youth and people of Nashua in memory of Holman's parents and was also partially funded by the federal Works Progress Administration (WPA) during the Great Depression. The stadium has been home to

71

many baseball teams and is currently the home of the Nashua Silver Knights of the Futures Collegiate Baseball League.

The stadium was also home to several minor-league affiliates of Major League Baseball organizations, beginning with the Nashua Dodgers, affiliated with the Brooklyn Dodgers. Holman also hosted the first integrated baseball team in the modern era when Roy Campanella and Don Newcombe played for the Nashua Dodgers in 1946.

The stadium has also hosted concerts by famous artists including, Aerosmith, The Beach Boys, Bob Dylan, Carlos Santana, and many others, and used by Nashua's local high school and Rivier University baseball teams.

One of the nation's leading photographers of airplanes resides in Nashua, **David Heath**. You can often find him at the Nashua Airport taking picture or having breakfast at the Airport Diner.

Mines Falls Park is a 325-acre park in the heart of the city. The site was purchased in 1969, and is bordered on the north by the Nashua River, and on the south by the millpond and power canal system. The name, "Mines Falls" dates from the early 18th century, when low quality lead was supposedly mined from the islands below the falls. In 1981 a regulation sized soccer playing field was added to the park, and other playing areas were later expanded to include additional soccer fields.

In 1992 the park's trails were designated part of the **New Hampshire Heritage Trail** system, which extends 130 miles along the Merrimack River from Massachusetts to Canada.

The best and cleanest barber shop in New Hampshire is located on East Pearl Street in Nashua and it is named **Empire Cuts**. Make an appointment with **Manny**, you will get the best haircut you ever had.

Greely Park is a public park occupying 125 acres in Nashua. The property was originally bought in 1801 by Joseph Greely, who passed it on to his son after his death. In 1908, John E. Cotton donated $5,000, an amount that was "matched by city funds", to change the Greely farm into a public park. The money was used to create a "stone and cement rest house, a fountain, a shallow pond, a gravel walk, and flower beds.

Greely Park hosts many citywide events, such as the Fairy Tale Festival Art Show, Halloween Fright Night, and in the spring and summer there are plays, movies, and music festivals. The park also features hiking trails, horseshoe pits, tennis courts, ball fields, a community gardening section. In 1999, American politician John McCain officially announced his candidacy for president of the United States to a crown of around 1,000 in Greely Park.

Attended by thousands, the annual S**t. Phillip Greek Food Festival** offers traditional Greek cuisine, Greek music, dance, and vender stalls during the festival. **Saint Phillip Greek Orthodox Church** has hosted the festival for more than 30 years, and being held in May, they are the first festival of the season every year.

Each year, over 30,000 gather for **Nashua's Annual Winter Stroll**. It begins with a candle lit procession from City Hall to the **Hunt Memorial Building** for the lighting of the city's Christmas tree. After the lighting, there are over 60 performances, animatronic animal rides, street venders, live ice sculpting/carving, music, food, and tons of fun.

Conway Arena houses Nashua's premiere ice skating rink. It has hosted many specialty events over the past 11 years including, charity tournaments, hockey tournaments, school field trips, scout outings, weddings, and birthday parties. A spacious, modern ice-skating rink, it features hockey and lessons plus an arcade, snack bar, and pro shop. Their summer programs offer many different kinds of clinics, including their Pro Ambitions Bruins Camp, designed to increase skill levels with almost 40 hours of on ice training.

MILFORD

ALL ABOUT MILFORD

Milford is a town in Hillsborough County on the Skowhegan River. Milford separated from neighboring Amherst in 1794, and like most towns named Milford in the United States, its name comes from the fact that it grew around a mill built on a ford on the Souhegan River. Its current population is 16,131 (2020) covering about 25.5 square miles and is the retail and manufacturing center of a multi town area known informally as the Souhegan Valley.

Milford was once home to numerous granite quarries, which produced a stone that was used, among other things, to make the pillars for the U.S. Treasury in Washington D.C.-pillars that can be seen on the back of the $10 bill. Its nickname, "The Granite Town", remains, although only one small quarry is in operation as of 2017.

Monson Village, now a part of Milford and Hollis, was the state's first inland colony settled as early as the 1730's. In 1741, the borders of Massachusetts and New Hampshire were established, and Monson became part of New Hampshire, incorporating in 1746. But the village never progressed, and gradually settlers moved away, and by the 1770s Monson was deserted. Today, Monson is a 280-acre historic site, and one of the most significant archeological sites in New England. There are trails, old foundations, cellar holes, wells, and the restored Joseph Gould homestead to transport you back to where about 300 o New Hampshire's first settlers lived and worked.

A stop on the **Underground Railroad**, Milford was the home of Harriet E. Wilson, who published the semi-autobiographical novel, "Our Ng: Or Sketches in the Life of a Free Black in 1859, the first novel by an African American woman published in North America.

PEOPLE OF SIGNIFICANCE - MILFORD

Harriet Wilson (b. 1825) was considered the first female, African-American of any gender to publish a novel on the North American continent when, in 1859, she deposited a copy of her novel in the Office of the Clerk of the U.S. District Court of Massachusetts. In it, she told the story of her own abandonment, her indentured servitude, and her fight or survival. She died at the age of 75 in Quincy, Mass.

Morgan Andrews (b. 1995) is an American soccer played in the National Women's Soccer League. She also represented the United States on numerous national teams from the under-15 to the under-23 levels. Morgan was twice named Gatorade National High School Player of the Year, and helped lead the USC Trojans to their second-ever NCAA College Cup Title in 2016.

Abby Hutchinson (b. 1829), descendant of the Pilgrims, came from a long line of musical ancestors. In 1839, Abby made her first appearance as a singer along with her parents and their thirteen children. In1843, the family visited New York City and took the New Yorkers by storm. Thereafter, they joined with the Abolitionists, and in their concerts sang ringing songs of freedom. Abby was also interested in the education of women, and was an earnest believer in women's suffrage.

Do You Know Milford?

The Milford Fish Hatchery was created in 1973 by the New Hampshire Fish and Game Department and covers 10.5 acres along the Souhegan River. The wildlife associated with the wetland around the area includes deer, turkey, grouse, coyote, muskrat and beaver. The field areas are annually stocked with pheasant each fall. The hatchery is open to the public, offering interactive educational exhibits, and nature trails constructed by the Milford Conservation Commission.

Milford's three-day **Great Pumpkin Festival** has been held every October for over 30 years, and draws thousands of visitors. This family friendly festival features a giant pumpkin weigh-in contest, pumpkin painting, carving, catapulting, and sales, scarecrow making, haunted trails, food vendors and live music. A craft fair is held upstairs in the Town Hall, featuring dozens of craft items, as well as rides and games for all ages.

Hanging in the belfry of Milford's Town Hall is an original **Paul Revere Bell No. 56,** cast in1802, and is likely the only bell in New Hampshire that has remained intact, never recast and never cracking. It was a gift from Perkins Nichols of Boston and Amherst in honor of the ordination of his friend the Rev. Humphrey Moore, Milford's first settled pastor. The bell is 30 inches high overall with a diameter at the shoulder of 16 inches, and a diameter at the mouth of almost 33 inches. It weighs approximately eight hundred pounds. Today, it chimes the hour every hour.

Monson was a town in Hillsborough County, and a part of Milford, that for reasons still unknown became abandoned in 1770. Its old roads are now walking trails that lead past the remnants of the original settlers' homes, with signs identifying those families who lived in them. Rumors have been heard of ghosts still walking the town, but the only building still standing is a restored house, which occasionally opens as a small museum of the village.

PETERBOROUGH

ALL ABOUT PETERBOROUGH

Peterborough is located thirty-eight miles west of Manchester, and 72 miles northwest of Boston. The main village of 39,000 (2020) is located along the Contoocook River, and its total population is 6,418 (2020). Granted by Massachusetts in 1737, Peterborough was first permanently settled in 1749, yet the town was attacked several times during the French and Indian War (1754-1763), but by 1759 there were fifty families settled. Like many southern New Hampshire towns, it was water that offered numerous sites for water mills, and Peterborough became a prosperous mill town. In 1810, the first cotton factory was established, and by1859 there were four additional factories, plus a woolen mill. Other industries included two paper mills, an iron foundry, a machine shop, a carriage factory, a shoe factory, seven saw mills, three gristmills, and a basket manufacturer (1875).

Peterborough has a total area of 38.4 square miles. Its highest point, and the highest point in Hillsborough County is the summit of South Pack Monadnock (2,290 ft.) in Miller State Park.

After being charged with heresy, Reverend Abiel Abbot came to Peterborough as minister to the Peterborough Unitarian Church in 1827, where he founded the town's first prep school, and the first free library in the U.S. The library started in the town's general store, which also served as the post office, but by 1890 there were 6,000 books, so the town built a new library that is still in use today.

PEOPLE OF SIGNIFICANCE - PETERBOROUGH

Marian MacDowell (b. 1857) was an American pianist and philanthropist. In 1907, she and her husband Edward MacDowell founded the MacDowell Colony for artists, one of the foremost cultural institutions in the United States. Through two world wars, and a Great Depression, the colony has cultivated the work of generations of musicians, writers, poets, sculptors, and visual artists. In 1896, she bought the Hillcrest Farm in Peterborough for their summer residence, and had a log studio built where her husband composed music. Realizing that artists could benefit from interacting with people from other disciplines, they developed plans where artists could come, live, and interact. In 1947, Marian stepped down from the Edward MacDowell Association, and died on August 23, 1956, in Los Angeles, California.

A resident of Peterborough, **Beth Krammes** is an American illustrator of children's books, winning the Golden Kite Award (2002), and the 2009 Caldecott Medal. She earned a BFA in painting from Syracuse, and a MAT in art education from the University of Massachusetts, Amherst. She has illustrated children's books since 1989.

Born in 1793, **Moses Cheney** was in the paper printing business, and also served as a conductor on the Underground Railroad from his home in Peterborough, where he hosted Frederick Douglass on several occasions. Cheney was the original printer of The Morning Star, an abolitionist Freewill Baptist newspaper. His son, Oren Cheney, was the founder and first president of Bates College in Maine.

Elting E. Morrison (b. 1909) was an American historian of technology, military biographer, author of non- fiction books and essayist. He was an MIT professor, and the founder of MIT's Science, Technology, and Society (STS) program. He earned a BA degree from Harvard in 1932, and an MA in 1934, returning in 1935-1937 as an assistant dean. In 1942, he published the biography of U.S. Admiral William Sims just a few months after the Pearl Harbor Attack, and it quickly became the standard scholarly biography. In 1948 Morrison became the director of the Theodore Roosevelt Research Project, which resulted in 8-volume work, The Letters of Theodore Roosevelt (1951-1954). Morrison died in Peterborough in 1995.

George Swinnerton Parker (b. 1866) was an American game designer and businessman who founded the Geo. S. Parker Company, and Parker Brothers. He published his first game, Banking, in 1883 at the age of 16. The game was so popular among family and friends that his brother Charles urged him to publish it. He spent $40 to make 500 sets of Banking, and eventually sold all but 12, making a profit of $100. During the Great Depression, when companies were going out of business, Parker Brothers released a new board game named Monopoly. It was an instant success. The company continued to grow with such games as, Risk, sorry, and Clue-a murder mystery game based on the house that Parker and his wife owned in Peterborough.

Do You Know Peterborough?

Established in 1933, **The Peterborough Players** brings quality professional theater productions to Peterborough. Performances are held in a small theater that has been converted from a historic barn dating back to the 18th century at **Stearns Farm**, just a few miles from downtown Peterborough. As one of the country's oldest summer stock companies, it offers a state of the art 250 seat, air conditioned theater, and a leading destination for theater in the region.

Miller State Park sits at the flank and nearly 3,000 ft. summit of New Hampshire's **Pack Monadnock**, and the state's oldest state park. As well as picnicking, and outdoor activities, Miller State Park also offers hiking trails, with three of the main hiking trails ascending to the summit of Pack Monadnock. Perhaps the most well-known of the trails is the Wapack Trail, extending a total of twenty-one miles from Watatic to North Pack Monadnock.

For more than 20 years, the **Mariposa Museum and World Cultural Center** has explored the multi-cultural diversity throughout the world. Located in the historic red-brick Baptist Church in the center of Peterborough, the museum offers a hands-on adventure celebrating cultures and people from around the globe. Exhibits are mostly interactive, and include the costume and puppet alcove and the top-floor musical instrument collection, where visitors are encouraged to experiment.

The Peterborough Diner still stands today as a historic Worcester Car Diner from the 1950's. Well known for being the region's first Worcester Lunch Car, it embraces its historical character, while meeting the challenges of the present day. Its open seven days a week for both breakfast and lunch, from seven in the morning until two in the afternoon.

The Peterborough Basket Company is the oldest continuous manufacturer of baskets in the U.S. Since 1854, the Peterborough Basket Co. has been producing hand-woven, hardwood baskets, made from Appalachian White Ash. Unfortunately, the factory will be producing its last basket in the summer/fall of 2022.

CAN YOU IDENTIFY THIS PHOTO? This is an artist cottage in the MacDowell Colony, a venerable organization that provides support and residencies for artists. Peterborough is considered a regional hub for arts and culture.

MERRIMACK

ALL ABOUT MERRIMACK

Merrimack is a Native American term meaning sturgeon, a type of fish. The Pennacook people named the Merrimack River after this fish because of the vast population that once existed there. When the town was incorporated in 1746, it took the name of the river, European settlers first came to the area in the late 17th century when the area was still in dispute between the Province of New Hampshire and Massachusetts Bay Colony. On April 2, 1746, Governor Benning Wentworth signed a charter establishing that the land from Pennachuck Brook to the Souhegan River became the town of Merrymack. At that time, there were fewer than 50 families living there.

The nineteenth century saw much growth in Merrimack. The meetinghouse was too small, and needed to be closer to the center of town;

two new churched were built; the Boston and Maine Railroad laid tracks through the town, with several stations operating into the mid-20th century, when the advent of the automobile transformed the town from a largely agricultural community to a bedroom community of Boston and nearby cities in New Hampshire.

Merrimack has a total area of 33.4 square miles, with its highest point being an unnamed hill in the northwest part of town that reaches 512 ft. Its current population is 26,632 (2020), and shadows of the former village that now make Merrimack still exist, but the boundaries and exact are unclear due to the expansion of urban development in the latter half of the 20th century.

The area of town near Naticook Lake takes its name from Matthew Thornton, one of the signers of the Declaration of Independence who lived in Merrimack, and is buried in a cemetery near the intersection of Daniel Webster Highway and Greely Street.

PEOPLE OF SIGNIFICANCE - MERRIMACK

Matthew Thornton (b. 1714) was a founding father of the United States who signed the Declaration of Independence as a representative of New Hampshire. His family emigrated from Ireland when he was three years old, and he later completed his studies in medicine at Leicester, and established a practice in Londonderry, New Hampshire. He was appointed surgeon to the New Hampshire Militia, served in the New Hampshire Provisional Assembly, had commissions as Justice of the Peace, and served as a colonel in the militia, resigning in 1779.

Thornton retired from medical practice, and in 1780 moved to Merrimack where he farmed and operated Thornton's Ferry with his family. Although he never attended law school, he served as a judge on the New Hampshire Superior Court from 1776-1782. Matthew Thornton died at age 90, and is buried in Thornton cemetery in Merrimack. His cenotaph reads: "Honest Man."

Born October 30, 1896, **Forrest Percival Sherman** was an admiral in the U.S. Navy, and the youngest person to serve as Chief of Naval Operations. The Forrest Sherman-class destroyer was named for him. Born in Merrimack, Sherman was a member of the U.S. Naval Academy class of 1918. Sherman held many ranks and commands in the years ahead, and in 1942 was awarded the Navy Cross for his extraordinary heroism during the opening days of the South Pacific Operation. In 1943 now Rear Admiral Sherman was assigned as Deputy Chief of Staff to the Pacific Fleet Commander, Admiral Chester W. Nimitz. Admiral Forrest Sherman died on July 22, 1951 in Naples, Italy, and is buried in Arlington National Cemetery.

Walter Kittredge (b. 1834) was born in Merrimack, the tenth of eleven children. He was a self-taught musician who played the violin, the melodeon, and the seraphine, a type of reed-like organ. He toured solo, and with the Hutchinson Family Troupe. Over his career he wrote over 500 songs, many of them dealing with the American Civil War. Perhaps his most famous song, "Tenting on the Old Campground", also known as "Tenting Tonight", was sung by both sides of the war and is known throughout the world. He offered the song to a Boston publisher for $15, but was rejected. When it was published several months later, ten thousand copies were sold within the first three months. Kittredge stated that he "actually saw the whole scene as described in the song" during a sleepless night. He died in his birthplace, a house on Bedford Road, Merrimack, in 1905.

DO YOU KNOW MERRIMACK?

The **Anheuser-Bush Brewery** in Merrimack celebrated its 50th anniversary of brewing beer in New Hampshire in 2020. When it first opened in 1970, the brewery brewed two brands. Now, it brews twenty distinct brands. Over the past 50 years, the Merrimack brewery has won more Global Budweiser Cups than any of its sister breweries, and the Merrimack facility has reduced water usage at the brewery by 66% since 2000. The brewery serves all of New England, and its 531 employees can package 8 million 12 ounce servings in just 24 hours. The brewery offers tours of 1.5 hours, a hospitality room, and a gift shop. Unfortunately, the Merrimack brewery was once the training facility of the world famous Clydesdale horses, but has since moved it to Warm Springs Ranch, near Boonville, Missouri. Anheuser Bush owns a total of about 250 Clydesdales kept at various locations throughout the United States, one of the largest herds of Clydesdales in the world.

The **Rock'n Ribfest** was an annual event held from 2003 through 2018, the proceeds of which benefitted many local charities. In 2019 the event was hosted by the Merrimack Rotary Club and renamed the **Great American Ribfest and Food Truck Festival**, held on the grounds of Anheuser-Bush.

Thomas Moore College is a private, Roman Catholic Liberal Arts college in Merrimack. It emphasizes classical education in the Catholic intellectual tradition, and is named after Saint Thomas More. Founded in 1978, the curriculum centers on the direct reading of foundational works of Western culture. In 2010, the college started a program of teaching students practical skills in art and music, using the medieval guild system as a model. From 2012 to 2021, the college was awarded an "A" rating from the American Council of Trustees and Alumni, and in 2021 the Young Americans Foundation named Thomas More College one of the top conservative schools in the U.S.

Opened in 2012, the **Merrimack Premium Outlets** is a 560,000 square foot, outdoor retail mall area with over 100 stores and restaurants. A frequent tour bus destination, the mall includes several upscale outlets, such as Barbour, Coach, Michael Kors, Guess, True Religion, and Lucky Brand Jeans. Larger anchor-type stores include Polo, Ralph Lauren, Saks Fifth Avenue, Bloomingdales Outlet, and Banana Republic factory store.

Twin Bridge Park is a 27-acre property situated at the heart of Merrimack's Town Center. The park is named for its historical significance, as the two bridges were used to cross the brook during the colonial era. The mammoth stones that were used to anchor the original bridges can still be seen today at the Baboosic Brook which borders the park's north and east areas. The park offers many walking paths, a play area known as **Kids Kove,** a baseball field, and a basketball half-court.

CAN YOU IDENTIFY THIS PHOTO? This is a depiction of Matthew Thornton, who signed the Declaration of Independence as a representative of New Hampshire.

MERRIMACK COUNTY

Merrimack County is a county in the south-central part of New Hampshire. Named for the Merrimack River, Merrimack County is the third most populous county in New Hampshire, with a population of 153,808 (2020), and was organized in 1823 from parts of Hillsborough and Rockingham counties. Its total area is 956 square miles, and its highest peak is Mt. Kearsarge at 2,937 feet. Its county seat is Concord, the state capital, and as of 2,000, the population density was 146 people per square mile, and in 2010, the center of population of New Hampshire was located in Merrimack County, in the town of Pembrok

CONCORD

ALL ABOUT CONCORD

The city of Concord is Merrimack County's largest city and serves as the state's capital. Its population of 43,976 makes it the third largest city in the state behind Manchester and Nashua.

The area that would become Concord was originally settled by Native Americans called the 'Pennacook'. The area was first settled by Europeans in 1659, as Penacook after the Abenaki word "pannukog" meaning "bend in the river", referencing the steep bends of the Merrimack River through the area. It was renamed "Concord" in 1765 by Governor Benning Wentworth.

Concord's central geographical location made it a logical choice for the state's capital, particularly after a canal and lock system was opened in 1807 which connected Concord with Boston by was of the Middlesex canal. Concord's 1819 State House is the oldest capital in the nation in which the state's legislative branches meet in their original chambers. The State House was designed by architect, Stuart Park, on land sold to the state by local Quakers. The city is home to The University of New Hampshire School of Law, New Hampshire's only law school, St. Paul's School, a private preparatory school, New Hampshire Police Academy, and the New Hampshire Fire Academy. Concord's Old North Cemetery is the final resting place of Franklin Pierce, the 14th President of the United States.

PEOPLE OF SIGNIFICANCE - CONCORD

Emma Elizabeth Brown (b. 1847) was an American of prose, poetry, and biographies. Her father, John Frost Brown was a leading bookseller in Concord, and an ardent lover of beauty. During her girlhood, she took long walks with him and taught her to note the changing beauties of nature, which she later reproduced on both canvass and page. She contributed to the Atlantic Monthly, The Aldine, the Living Age, and others, as well as biographies of Washington, Grant, Garfield, and Oliver Wendell Holmes.

Franklin Pierce (b. 1804) was the 14th President of the United States, serving from March 4th 1853-March 4th, 1857. He died October 8th, 1869, and is buried in the Old North Cemetery in Concord. He served in both the New Hampshire Militia, and the United States Army, rising to the rank of colonel (militia), and Brigadier General (Army).

His tenure as president was a contentious one, trying to satisfy diverse elements of the Democratic Party, which ultimately abandoned him. His bid for a second term failed, and his reputation suffered as he became a vocal critic of Abraham Lincoln.

Levi Hutchins (b. 1761) was an American clockmaker, and inventor of the first American alarm clock. Levi and his two brothers set up shop on Main Street, and in 1787 he created his alarm clock, housed in a 29"x14" wooden cabinet with mirrored doors, and had an extra gear that rang an attached bell at 4 a.m. In 1807 the brothers dissolved their partnership. But Hutchins continued to build brass clocks as well as surveying compasses for another 20 years.

David Souter (b. 1939) was a retired associate justice of the Supreme Court, serving from October 1990 to his retirement in June 2009. Appointed by President George H.W. Bush, Souter sat on both the Rehnquist and Roberts courts. After his retirement from the court, he was succeeded by Sonia Sotomayor, but continued to hear cases by designation at the circuit court level.

Christa McAuliffe (b. 1948) was an American teacher and astronaut from Concord who was killed on the Space Shuttle Challenger, where she was serving as a payload specialist. McAuliffe was selected from more than 11,000 applicants to the NASA Teacher in Space project, and was scheduled to become the first teacher to fly in space. On January 28, 1986 the shuttle broke apart 1 minute 13 seconds after launch, resulting in the loss of all on board. She was posthumously awarded the Congressional Space Medal of Honor in 2,004.

Do You Know Concord?

McAuliffe-Shepard Discovery Center is a 45,000 square foot museum memorial to Alan Shepard and Crista McAuliffe, whose mission is to inspire every generation to reach for the stars. The center explores astronomy and aviation, with interactive exhibits, simulations, planetary observatory, and more. Exhibits include a full-sized replica of a Mercury-Redstone rocket, a full-dome digital planetarium, an observatory, and a full complement of on and offsite educational programs.

Capitol Center for the Arts is an entertainment venue that features a 1,304-seat theater designed with an Egyptian motif. It is equipped to stage major Broadway shows, and has played host to the Billy Joel musical, "Movin' Out," pianist George Winston, and humorist David Sedaris.

New Hampshire Historical Society holds an extensive collection of objects and archives related to New Hampshire history. Located at 6 Eagle Square, Concord, NH, the Historical Society has been preserving the state's past since 1823.

Carter Hill Orchard is a family owned and operated farm that includes hiking trails, an on-site bakery, a country store, as well as an observation tower that offers great views of the occasional raptor and the mountains of New Hampshire. Depending on the season, the orchard has cantaloupe, watermelon, pears, plums, raspberries, blueberries, and over ten varieties of apples.

CANTERBURY

ALL ABOUT CANTERBURY

With nearly 700 acres or forests, nature trails, and ponds, Canterbury is a definite point of interest in Merrimack County. First granted in 1727, the town was named for William Wake, Archbishop of Canterbury. The town was originally a fort or trading post where the Penacook Indians came to trade. The 2019 Census estimate for Canterbury was 2,464 residents, with approximately 56.1 persons per square mile of land area. It's perhaps best known for its 25 original, and 4 reconstructed Shaker buildings. Built in 1792, the community once housed 260 (1840) villagers, and by 1850 the site contained 3,000 acres with a community of 300 housed in a hundred buildings. Declared a National Historic Landmark in 1993, this site preserves the heritage of the Canterbury Shakers. The community of the United Society of Believers, known as the Shaking Quakers or Shakers, because of their use of dance in worship is today an outdoor museum and National

Historic Landmark. The biggest attraction in Canterbury is the Shaker village, where they made their living by farming, selling seeds, herbs and herbal medicines, and by manufacturing textiles, pails, brooms, and other unique products. The last resident, Sister Ethel Hudson, died in 1992, and the site is now a museum founded in 1969 under permanent conservation easement.

Canterbury has an active historical society hosting events throughout the year, and maintaining the Elizabeth Houser Museum in the Old Center Schoolhouse (original one-room schoolhouse) as well as an archive of Canterbury-related materials dating to the early 18th century. Among notable works in the archive are the Lither Cody Collection of glass negatives, documenting classic life in New England.

PEOPLE OF SIGNIFICANCE - CANTERBURY

Abiel Foster (b. 1735) was an American clergyman and politician from Canterbury, Hew Hampshire. He was a member of the 4th and 5th Congress of the Confederation from New Hampshire; member of the U.S. House of Representatives from New Hampshire; member of the New Hampshire Senate, and president of the New Hampshire Senate. He died in 1806, and is interred at the Center Cemetery, Canterbury, NH.

Stephen Symonds Foster (b.1809) was a radical American abolitionist, noted for his aggressive style of public speaking, and for his stance against those in the church who failed to fight slavery, and his marriage to Abby Kelley brought his activism to bear on women's rights. Foster helped establish the New Hampshire Anti-Slavery Society, writing many anti-slavery tracts and in 1843, publishing, *The Brotherhood of Thieves; Or a True Picture of the American Church and Clergy: A Letter to Nathaniel Barney of Nantucket*. The book was widely discussed, and met with protest and critical response. He also formed a link on the Underground Railroad, and helped fugitive slaves reach Canada and freedom.

Do You Know Canterbury?

Originally a militia timber fort and trading post of Captain Jeremiah Clough located on a hill near the **Canterbury Center.** There were several garrison houses or stockades in the area as late as 1758. Today, there are multiple four season recreational opportunities in Canterbury, including canoeing, kayaking, swimming, and fishing with hiking trails and conservation areas open to the public. In the winter months, the NH-Snow Shakers snowmobile club operates a clubhouse and large network of trails for snowmobile enthusiasts and cross- country skiers.

As of 1920 there were only 12 Shaker communities in the United States. As of 2019, there is only one active **Shaker Village.** Consequently, many of the other settlements are now museums. Shaker Village in Canterbury is an internationally known historic site. It was one of a number of Shaker communities founded in the 19th century, and is one of the most intact and authentic surviving Shaker community sites.

WILMOT

All About Wilmot

Welcome to the rural community of Wilmot. Wilmot is a small town (1,407) (2020) in Merrimack County. Originally a part of New London, the town took its name from Dr. James Wilmot, an English clergyman who spoke out against England's treatment of the American colonies. The town has a total area of 29.6 square miles of land, and 0.2 square miles or 0.70% are water. The entire town is part of the Merrimack River watershed and is dotted with several large ponds. On its southern border is Mount Kearsarge, with an elevation of 2,931 feet. It is the highest point in town, and in Merrimack County. Winslow State Park at the northern foot of the mountain provides two access trails to the summit. The park and the Winslow Trail are named for Captain John Winslow, commander of the USS Kearsarge, which in June 1864 sank the CSS Alabama in the English Channel in a famous Civil War battle.

PEOPLE OF SIGNIFICANCE - WILMOT

Donald Hall (b. 1928) is an American poet, writer, editor, and literary critic. The author of over 50 books across several genres, including 22 volumes of verse, he is a graduate of Phillips Exeter Academy, Harvard, and Oxford. Early on, he was the first poetry editor of the Paris Review, and was noted for interviewing poets and other authors on their craft. In June 2006, Hall was appointed as the Library of Congress's 14th Poet Laureate Consultant in Poetry, better known as "Poet Laureate of the United States". Donald Hall has taught at Stanford University, Bennington College, and the University of Michigan, and in 2010 was awarded the National Medal of Arts by President Obama.

DO YOU KNOW WILMOT?

Wilmot is dotted with numerous brooks and ponds noted for their fishing and abundant plant life. **Eagle Pond** was made famous by Donald Hall's "Seasons at Eagle Pond", which referenced the pond and its surrounding landscape. **Bog Mountain in Gile State Forest** offers a number of moderately challenging trails with some spectacular views. **Winslow State Park** is located on the northwest slope of Mt. Kearsarge, with outstanding views of the White Mountains to the north and the taller of the southern and central Vermont peaks.

NEW LONDON

ALL ABOUT NEW LONDON

New London is considered one of the best places to live in New Hampshire. The town offers a variety of unique retail shops, fine dining, lodging, and entertainment, and in the summer months it provides concerts, festivals, parades, and popular plays in The Barn Playhouse. Winter activities include skiing at nearby Mt. Sunapee, snowshoeing, snowmobiling, skating, and miles of cross country skiing, making it a year round destination. Incorporated in 1779, New London is situated just north of Concord in Merrimack County.

The town common is surrounded by the **New London Inn** and the tree-lined streets of **Colby Sawyer College**. The college was founded as a coeducational academy in 1837, and sits on a 200-acre campus. The college boasts a number of distinguished alumni, among whom is the noted children's author **Tomie DePaola**, who worked at Colby Sawyer as an associate professor, designer, technical director in the speech and theater department, and as a writer for the **Children's Theater Project**.

The town has a population of 4,400 as of the 2020 census, covering about 25.42 square miles of land. Nearly all the original settlers came from Massachusetts, and by 1779 there were 16 families who petitioned the General Court to incorporate as the town of "New London," after London, England. The first town meeting was held August 3, 1779.

PEOPLE OF SIGNIFICANCE — NEW LONDON

Julia Amanda Sargent Wood (b. 1825), an American sentimental writer who produced an astonishing number of poems, stories, sketches, and novels, began writing early in life, but didn't publish until she was in her 40's. Many of Wood's novels were Catholic themed, and believed that women should work towards suppression of the divorce laws.

DO YOU KNOW NEW LONDON?

Lake Sunapee (4,125 acres), a cold and warm water fishery, attracts many people in the summer for its recreational activities. Little Sunapee Lake is on the west side of town, and **Pleasant Lake** is on the east side and features a public beach access, and fireworks on the 4th of July.

New London Barn Playhouse, a prominent summer stock small professional theater, is New Hampshire's oldest summer theater and produces musicals and dramas to sold-out crowds. It has been listed in the New Hampshire Register of Historic Places since 2006.

Mount Sunapee Resort is about 20 minutes south of town, and provides skiing and riding in the winter, and hiking, zip lining, rock climbing, and Segway tours in the summer.

The Ice House Museum houses a collection of automobiles and Americana. **The New London Historical Society** offers guided tours of its carriage and sleigh museum, and its 19th century village depicting rural New England life.

LOUDON

ALL ABOUT LOUDON

The town of Loudon was originally incorporated by Governor John Wentworth on January 23, 1773. It was originally formed o territory taken from Canterbury, and the new town was named IN HONOR OF JOHN CAMPBELL, 4TH EARL of Louden, a Scottish soldier and leader of British military forces in North America during the French and Indian War. Louden also helped to establish an independent company of colonial militia called Roger's Rangers. One of Lord Loudon's aides, John Louden McAdam, invented a new process called "macadamizing" for building roads more durable and less muddy than soil-based roads. The town itself has a total area of 46.7 square miles, and its highest point is near its northern border, where an unnamed summit just north of the location known as Sabattus Heights reaches1,050 feet above sea level. The main village in town is located along the Suncook River at the southern terminus of New Hampshire Route 129.

PEOPLE OF SIGNIFICANCE - LOUDON

Sir John Wentworth (b. 1737), 1st Baronet, was the British Colonial Governor of New Hampshire at the time of the American Revolution. Under Wentworth's administration, the growing province was divided into five counties, and Wentworth was responsible for naming them, choosing names of current British leaders and after one of his distant relatives. He developed a system of roads between the major population centers in the province, and is reported to have constructed more than 200 miles of new roads.

DO YOU KNOW LOUDON?

New Hampshire Motor Speedway is a 1.058-mile oval speedway located in Loudon. The speedway has hosted NASCAR racing annually since 1990, as well as the longest running motorcycle race in North America, The Loudon Classic. Nicknamed "The Magic Mile', the speedway is often converted into a 1.6-mile road course which includes much of the oval. The track is currently one of eight major NASCAR tracks owned and operated by Speedway Motorsports. With a seating capacity of 76,000 it is not only the largest speedway in New England, but the largest sports and entertainment venue of this type in the region.

HENNIKER

ALL ABOUT HENNIKER

The area was first known as "Number Six" in a line of settlements running between the Merrimack and Connecticut rivers. In 1752, the "Masonian Proprietors" granted the land to Andrew Todd, who called it "Todd's Town". Incorporated in 1768 by Governor John Wentworth, the town was named for Sir John Henniker, a London merchant of leather and fur with shipping interests in Boston and Portsmouth.

Interestingly, the 19th century had a high rate of congenital deafness, and its own sign language, which may have played a significant role in the emergence of American Sign Language. Currently, the total population of Henniker is around 6,185, as of the 2020 census, and is located along the Contoocook River. Over its history, various mills operated by water power on the Contoocook River including a woolen factory. But the mills were closed in 1959 by the Hopkinton-Everett Lakes Flood Control Project.

PEOPLE OF SIGNIFICANCE - HENNIKER

Amy Marcy Cheney Beach (b.1867) was an American composer and pianist, and the first successful American female composer of large scale art music. Her "Gaelic Symphony" premiered by the Boston Symphony Orchestra in 1896, and was the first symphony composed and published by an American woman.

Mary Wilson Wallace (b. 1720), better known as Ocean Born Mary, is a folklore figure of New England. Mary was born on a ship in the Atlantic Ocean. During the voyage, the ship was reportedly taken over by pirates who threatened to loot it and sink it with all on board. When the pirate captain heard the cry of an infant, he went below to discover Mrs. Wilson holding her newborn daughter. He apparently told Mrs. Wilson that if she would allow him to name the baby, he would spare the ship and allow them to depart peacefully. Mrs. Wilson agreed, and the pirates departed.

Mary's claim to fame, however, is as a reputed ghost. The story of the haunting was begun by Louis Roy, who owned the Wallace House in the 1930s. He claimed that the same pirate captain who spared her ship reunited with her in widowhood, and she took him into her home to care for him in his old age. Allegedly, the captain was murdered under Mary's roof, and she buried him and his treasure under the hearthstone. Her ghost was said to haunt the house in order to protect the hidden treasure.

Kristen Ulmer (b. 1966) is a former professional skier, whose professional career lasted for almost two decades. Ulmer was not only on the U.S. Ski Team, but starred in over 20 ski movies, and was named the best female big mountain extreme skier in the world from 1990-2001. She is known for jumping off up to 70'cliffs, throwing flips, and for ski mountaineering feats such as the first female descent of Wyoming's Grand Teton in 1997. She retired from professional athletics in 2003.

Do You Know Henniker?

Pat's Peak is an independent alpine ski resort located in Henniker, New Hampshire. Opened in 1963, it has a vertical drop of 770 feet, and covers about two hundred acres, with about 103 acres that are skiable. In 2013-14, Pat's Peak opened an expansion on the east side of Craney Hill, named Cascade Basin, and it includes a triple chair lift covering 370 vertical feet. "Ski Magazine" has said it has the best slalom skiing terrain in New Hampshire.

New England College is a private liberal arts college in Henniker, with an enrollment of 4,327 students. Founded in 1946, New England College was established to serve the needs of servicemen and women attending college on the G.I. Bill after World War II. The 225 acre campus features 30 buildings, many of which feature the white clapboard-style or brick midcentury architecture. The campus is known throughout New England for promoting environmental education initiatives, and offers 9 associate degree programs, 37 bachelor degree programs, 12 graduate degree programs and one doctoral degree program. New England College has been publicly recognized by "Time Magazine" as one of the top 25 colleges in the nation that have diversified their student body the most since 1990.

CAN YOU IDENTIFY THIS PHOTO? The Labrie Family Skate at Puddle Dock Pond, on the 10-acre campus of the Strawbery Banke Museum in Portsmouth.

ROCKINGHAM COUNTY

With a population of 314,176 (2020), Rockingham County, New Hampshire is the second most populous county in the state, and per the 2020 census, it was New Hampshire's fastest growing county from 2010-2020. It covers about 792.2 square miles, about 99.9 square miles of which are water.

The area that is today Rockingham County was first settled by Europeans moving north from the Plymouth Colony as early as 1623 and was tightly linked with Massachusetts until New Hampshire became a separate colony in 1679, but counties were not introduced until 1769. Rockingham was one of the five original counties for the colony, and was named for Charles Watson Wentworth, 2nd Marquess of Rockingham, who had been Prime Minister from 1765-1766. Exeter became the county seat in 1771, but the county court facilities were moved to Brentwood, a rural town adjacent to Exeter.

Rockingham County occupies the southeast corner of the state, and contains the state's easternmost point. The county contains all of New Hampshire's Atlantic Coast, which is approximately 18 miles, the shortest ocean coastline of any state in the U.S., and its highest point is Nottingham Mountain, at 1,340 ft. in Deerfield.

PORTSMOUTH

ALL ABOUT PORTSMOUTH

Portsmouth is an historic, seaport city in Rockingham County, with a total area of 15.7 square miles, and a population of 21,956 as of the 2020 census. It is a popular summer tourist destination on the Piscataqua River, bordering the state of Maine.

The Abenaki and Algonquian Indians inhabited the territory of coastal New Hampshire for thousands of years before European contact. The first known European to explore and write about the area was Martin Pring in 1603. Since the Piscataqua River is a tidal estuary with a swift current, it forms a good natural harbor, and the west bank of the harbor was settled by European colonists in 1630, and named Strawberry Banke after the many wild strawberries growing there. The village was protected by Fort William and Mary on what is now New Castle Island. The port's principle businesses were fishing, lumber and shipbuilding, and it prospered. Enslaved Africans were imported as laborers as early as 1645, and were integral to building the city's prosperity. At the town's incorporation in 1653, it was named "Portsmouth" in honor of the colony's founder, John Mason, who had been captain of the English Port of Portsmouth, Hampshire, after which New Hampshire is named. When Queen Anne's War ended in 1712, Governor Joseph Dudley selected the town to host negotiations for the 1713 Treaty of Portsmouth, which temporarily ended hostilities between the Abenaki Indians and the colonies of Massachusetts Bay and New Hampshire.

In the lead-up to the Revolution, Paul Revere rode to Portsmouth to warn that the British Navy was coming to capture the fort. Although Fort William and Mart protected the harbor, the Patriot Government moved the capital inland to Exeter. African Americans helped defend Portsmouth and New England during the war, and in 1779 nineteen enslaved African Americans from Portsmouth petitioned the state government to abolish slavery in recognition or their contributions, and in keeping with the principles of the Revolution. Their petition was not answered, but New Hampshire later abolished slavery.

Once one of the nation's busiest ports and shipbuilding cities, Portsmouth expressed its wealth in fine architecture. It has significant examples of Colonial Georgian, and Federal style houses, some of which are now museums. A devastating fire torched 244 buildings in 1813, and a fire district was created that required all buildings within its boundaries to be built of brick with slate roofs; this created the downtown's distinctive appearance. In the 20th Century, the city founded a Historic District Commission to protect much of the city's irreplaceable architectural legacy, and in 2008, the National Trust for Historic Preservation named Portsmouth one of the "Dozen Distinctive Destinations". Currently, the compact and easily walkable downtown on the waterfront draws tourists and artists, who each summer throng the cafes, restaurants and shops around Market Square.

PEOPLE OF SIGNIFICANCE - PORTSMOUTH

Tom Rush (b. 1941) is an American singer and songwriter who began performing in 1961, while studying at Harvard University majoring in English Literature. He's the son of a teacher, whose early recordings are versions of Lowland Scots, and Appalachian folk songs. Rush is credited by Rolling Stone magazine as ushering in the era of the singer-songwriter, while also performing the songs of Joni Mitchell, Jackson Browne, James Taylor, helping them to gain recognition early in their careers. On December 28th, 2012 appeared at Boston Symphony Hall to celebrate fifty years in the music business.

Born in 1782, **Daniel Webster** established a successful legal practice in Portsmouth, New Hampshire after graduating from Dartmouth College. He won election to the United States House of Representatives, where he served as a leader of the Federalist Party. After serving two terms, he left office and relocated to Boston where he became a leading attorney before The Supreme Court of the United States. Webster returned to the House in 1823 and became a key supporter of President John Quincy Adams, and in 1827 won election to the United States Senate. Webster is widely regarded as an important and talented attorney, orator, and politician, but historians have mixed opinions on his ability as a national leader.

Oney Judge (b. 1773) was a woman of mixed races who was enslaved to the Washington family at Mount Vernon and later at the President's house in Philadelphia. In her early 20's, she ran away becoming a fugitive slave, where she fled to New Hampshire and married, had children, and converted to Christianity. She thought she had found haven in Portsmouth, New Hampshire, but was recognized by Elizabeth Langdon, the daughter of Senator John Langdon. Washington knew of Judge's whereabouts, but was told that and attempt at abduction could cause a riot by the supporters of abolition. She did offer to return voluntarily to the Washington's if they would guarantee to free her following their deaths. In freedom, Judge learned to read, and became a Christian. She and her husband had fewer than 7 years together before he died in 1803. Oney Judge died February 25, 1848 at age 75.

Edmund March Blunt (b. 1770) was an American navigator, author, and publisher. He established a nautical book and chart publishing firm that became the largest publishing firm in the early 19th century. In 1796, he published "American Coastal Pilot", which described every port of the United States, as well as creating a map of what is now the Federated States of Micronesia. Blunt expanded his chart coverage into the Pacific Ocean, and in 1857 into the Indian Ocean. From 1819 to 1826, he conducted surveys of the Bahama Islands and the Nantucket Shoals, and made the first accurate survey of the New York harbor. Blunt died in 1862 at age 92.

Do You Know Portsmouth?

Membership libraries were first created in the 18th century to elevate the educational resources available to the community. **The Portsmouth Athenaeum** is such a private library, museum, and art gallery opened to the public at certain times. The name is derived from the Greek god, Athena, goddess of wisdom, and the classical temple of the arts and sciences named to honor her. The Athenaeum maintains a library of over 40,000 volumes and an archive of manuscripts, photographs, and objects relating to local history, and sponsors exhibitions, concerts, lectures, and other educational and cultural programs. The building, dating back to1805, was listed on the National Register of Historic places in 1973.

North Church, built in 1657, sits in Market Square across from the Athenaeum, and prominent members included Daniel Webster, John

Langdon, and William Whipple. President George Washington attended a service during his visit to New Hampshire in 1789. Members were required to purchase pews, and slave owners had to purchase extra pews for their slaves. Although the structure went through many changes over the years, the clock, bell, and furnishings continued to be used. A new organ was added in 1890, and its bell was used to signal the community's 9 P.M. curfew from the 1700s into the 1900s.

Strawberry Banke is an outdoor history museum located in the historic district of Portsmouth. It is the oldest neighborhood in New Hampshire settled by Europeans, and the earliest neighborhood remaining in present day Portsmouth. It features more than 37 restored buildings built between the 17th and 19th centuries in the Colonial, Georgian, and Federal style architecture. The neighborhood dates back to 1630, when Captain Walter Neale chose the area to build a settlement, naming it after the wild strawberries growing along the Piscataqua River. Strawberry Banke opened as a museum in 1965.

The Portsmouth African Burying Ground is a memorial park in Portsmouth. The park sits on top of an 18th century gravesite containing almost 200 freed and enslaved African people and is the only archeologically verified African burying ground for the time period in New England. The site was discovered in 2003, when construction workers discovered the buried, which included four men, one female, and one child. The rest were unable to be determined. The exact date of the first burial in the African Burial Ground is unknown, but maps dating back to 1705 have included the cemetery. The memorial park was unveiled on May 23, 2015, which also marked the date in which the eight exhumed individuals were reburied.

Portsmouth's **Black Heritage Trail** explores the history of Africans and African Americans who called Portsmouth home for more than 350 years. New Hampshire's African American heritage dates back to the arrival of Europeans, and much of that history began in 1645, centering on the state's only port at Portsmouth. As many as 700 blacks were by the Revolution, caught up in an active Northern slave market, while others were part of a little known free society. Africans and their descendants built communities and families, founded institutions, and served their town, state, and nation in many capacities, and the Black Heritage Trail promotes an awareness and appreciation of African American life.

99

Since 1962, **Portsmouth Harbor Cruises** have been a favorite of locals and tourists alike. Whether discussing the birdlife of the inland waterways, the folklore of The Isle of Shoals, the ship building of Portsmouth, or just the history and beauty of the seacoast and isles, Portsmouth Harbor Cruises are always interesting and informative.

The **John Paul Jones House** is a historic house in Portsmouth. Now a historic house museum and a National Historic Landmark, it is most significant as the only known surviving structure in the United States associated with American Revolutionary War Hero, John Paul Jones, who lived there in 1761-1782 when it was operated as a boarding house. Jones rented a room in the house while supervising construction of the ship "America". Originally built in 1758 by master housewright Hopestill Cheswell, a successful African American builder in the city, who owned it with his wife Sarah until his death in1776.

The **Music Hall** in Portsmouth is an 895 seat theater located on Chestnut Street in Portsmouth. Built in 1878, the music hall claims to be the oldest operating theater in New Hampshire, and the 14th oldest in the United States. Throughout the years, the Music Hall has brought the community opera, drama, dance, music, even hosting Buffalo Bill Cody and his Wild West Show, as well as its first moving pictures on Edison's Graphophone here in 1898.

The **USS Albacore** is a research submarine designed to test experimental features in modern submarines, some of which led to the high-speed silent operation used on today's modern submarines. At the Albacore Park in Portsmouth, visitors can go inside the submarine, look through the periscope, explore the control room, engineering spaces and bunkrooms. Tours through the submarine are self- guided, with a series of audio stations highlighting the Albacore's unique features, as well as recordings by former crew members. The Albacore was built by the Portsmouth Naval Shipyard, and served from 1953-1972, and in 1966, she set the record as the world's fastest sub having attained an underwater speed of nearly 40 miles per hour. In May of 1985, she settled into her final resting place on a concrete cradle in Albacore Park.

CAN YOU IDENTIFY THIS PHOTO? Wentworth by the Sea, Portsmouth's grand hotel.

EXETER

ALL ABOUT EXETER

Exeter, with a population of 16,049 (2020), was the county seat until 1997, when county offices were moved to neighboring Brentwood. Exeter is situated where the Exeter River becomes the tidal Squamscott River. The town has an area of 20 square miles, and was once the domain of the Swampscott people, a sub-tribe of the Pennacook nation. On April 3, 1638, the Reverend John Wheelwright, who had been exiled by the Massachusetts Bay Colony for sharing dissident religious views of his sister-in-law, Anne Hutchinson purchased the land where the future town of Exeter would grow. The minister took with him about 175 individuals to found the town of Exeter, named after Exeter in Devon, England. At that time, local government was linked with Massachusetts until New Hampshire became a separate colony in 1679.

Thomas Wilson established the town's first grist mill, and in 1647 Edward Gilman established the first sawmill, and by1651 Gilman had his own 50-ton sloop with which to conduct his business in lumber, staves, and masts. The Gilman Garrison House, a National Historic Landmark, and the American Independence Museum were both former homes of the Gilman family. The Gilman family also donated land on

101

which Phillips Exeter Academy stands, including the academy's original Yard, the oldest part of the campus.

Exeter suffered its last Indian raid in August 1723, and by 1725 the tribes had left the area. In 1774 the rebellious Provincial Congress began to meet in Exeter Town House after colonial Governor John Wentworth banned it from the colonial capital at Portsmouth. In July1775, the Provincial Congress had provincial records seized from royal officials in Portsmouth and brought to Exeter, making it New Hampshire's capital, an honor it held for 14 years.

PEOPLE OF SIGNIFICANCE - EXETER

John Phillips (b. 1719) was an early American educator, and the cofounder of Phillips Exeter Academy, along with his wife, Elizabeth Phillips. He was a major donor to Dartmouth College, Harvard College, and Princeton University. In 1741, Phillips moved to Exeter, where he headed a private school for a year, and afterwards a public school for a year. He and his wife founded Phillips Academy in Exeter in 1781, donating $134,000, and served as the president of the board of trustees until his death in 1795. His nephew, Samuel Phillips Jr. had founded the nearby Phillips Academy in Andover, Massachusetts, and inspired him to create his own school in Exeter. Both these schools are among the oldest, and most prestigious preparatory schools in the country.

John Irving, born John Wallace Blunt Jr., was born March 2, 1942, in Exeter. Irving achieved critical acclaim after the international success of *The World According to Garp* in 1978. Many of Irving's novels have been bestsellers, and he won the Academy Award for Best Adapted Screenplay in the 72nd Academy Awards (1999) for his script of "The Cider House Rules". Five of his novels have been adapted into films, with many set near Phillips Exeter Academy in Exeter.

Dan Brown is a noted author, born in Exeter on July 22, 1964. After graduating from Amherst, Brown dabbled with a music career, and in 1991 moved to Hollywood to pursue a career as a singer-songwriter and pianist. To support himself, he taught classes at Beverly Hills Preparatory School. In 1996, Brown quit teaching to become a full-time writer. His first three novels sold fewer than 10,000 copies in each of their first printings. His fourth novel, <u>The Da Vinci Code</u>, became a best-seller during its first week of release in 2003, and is one of the most popular books of all time. In 2005, Brown made Time Magazine's list of the 100 Most Influential People of the Year, with an estimated annual income of $76.5 million.

Born in Exeter in 1850, **Daniel Chester French** was an American sculptor, best known for his design of the monument statue of Abraham Lincoln in the Lincoln Memorial in Washington, D.C. His decision to pursue sculpting was said to have been influenced by Louisa May Alcott's sister May. French earned acclaim for The Minute Man, commissioned by Concord, Massachusetts and unveiled April 19, 1875, on the centenary of the Battle of Lexington and Concord. His reputation grew with his Statue of the Republic for the world's Columbian Exposition of 1893, bronze doors for the Boston Public Library, and Four Continents at the U.S. Custom House, New York (now the Alexander Hamilton U.S. Custom House). In 1917, French and a colleague designed the Pulitzer Prize gold metal presented to laureates. French died in Stockbridge, Massachusetts in 1931, at the age of 81. His summer home and studio is operated by the National Trust for Historic Preservation.

Ambrose Swasey (b. 1846) was an engineer, inventor, machinist, entrepreneur, and philanthropist from Exeter. He apprenticed as a machinist at the Exeter Machine Works, and was afterwards employed by Pratt & Whitney. As his career progressed, he developed new technique for making gear-tooth cutters, and in 1880 formed his own company where he performed engineering and machine development at the company. Swasey became interested in astronomical observatories and equipment, and in the quest for better optical telescopes, which were burgeoning at the time. In 1885, he completed work on the McCormick Observatory on the 45-foot dome, which was the largest in the world, and had a unique 3 shutter design. In 1887, he built the mount for the 36 inch refracting telescope at Lick Observatory, and in 1898 he manufactured a dividing engine for the U.S. Naval Observatory. From 1904-1905 he was the president of the American Society of Mechanical Engineers. Swasey died in 1937, and is buried in the Exeter Cemetery.

Do You Know Exeter?

The American Independence Museum is a historic house museum in Exeter. Its 1-acre campus includes two buildings: the **Ladd-Gilman House** built in 1721, and the **Folsom Tavern** built in 1775. The museum in 1991 after a rare copy of the Declaration of Independence known as a broadside was found in the Ladd-Gilman house, two hundred years after its arrival in Exeter. It was found by an electrician who was wiring a security system, when he pulled an old newspaper from under the attic floor. The electrician contacted the Society of the Cincinnati who had the document authenticated. The Society opened the museum to educate visitors about the Declaration and the Revolution. Exeter was the capital of New Hampshire when Colonel Samuel Folsom built his tavern in 1775. During the Revolutionary War, it was the site of many political debates and was a popular spot for the men in town. The New Hampshire chapter of the Society of the Cincinnati formed in the tavern in 1783, and George Washington stopped there in 1789 during a tour of the states

The Congregational Church in Exeter was gathered in 1638 by the Rev. John Wheelwright, following the expulsion from the Massachusetts Bay Colony. The current congregation is a merger of the former First Parish and Second Parish of Exeter. The second Parish split from the First Parish in the 1700s over theological differences. The two congregations reunited in 1920, and the church is now on the U.S. National Register of Historic Places. The current building was built in 1798, and can seat 400 people. It was designed by Ebenezer Clifford, and is believed to be the earliest church in the state to use a hip roof design, and its only entrances were through the projecting entrance bay, unlike earlier meetinghouses, which had entrances on three sides. Notable items inside the church include the pew in which Abraham Lincoln sat when he came to visit his son at the nearby Phillips Exeter Academy, and a portrait of Lincoln and a portrait of the Rev. Wheelwright. The church building also figures in John Irving's, "A Prayer for Owen Meany", as Irving grew up in the congregation.

The Swasey Parkway, was a gift to the town of Exeter from Ambrose Swasey in 1931. The Parkway follows the Squamscott River and is lined with trees and park benches for all to enjoy. The park is open from dawn to dusk, and provides a scenic setting for the Powder Keg

Beer and Chili Festival, held in October of each year. A pavilion, completed in 2007, hosts concerts on Thursday nights in the summer.

The Powder House was built in 1771, and can be seen across the river from Swazey Parkway. On December, 1812 the State Legislature passed a resolution empowering the governor to purchase a supply of powder, lead, and flints for the use of the state. Half the material was to be stored in Exeter. It is thought that a number of barrels were stored in The Powder House and used at the battle of Bunker Hill. The Powder House still stands today, and was refurbished in 1999.

SALEM

ALL ABOUT SALEM

First settled in1652, Salem was the "North Parish" of Methuen, Massachusetts. In 1741, when the boundary line between Massachusetts and New Hampshire was fixed, the "North Parish" became part of New Hampshire, and was given the name "Salem", taken from nearby Salem, Massachusetts. The town was incorporated in 1750 by colonial governor Benning Wentworth. The meetinghouse erected in 1738 still stands, eventually becoming the town hall of Salem before it was turned into the Salem Historical Society Museum.

Salem has a total area of 25.90 square miles, and boasts a population of 30,089 (2020). Located on Interstate 93, it is the first town in New Hampshire, which lacks sales tax. Salem has grown into a commercial hub, anchored by the Mall at Rockingham Park. In 1902, Canobie Lake Park opened, quickly becoming one of the leading resorts of its type in New England. Crowds from Massachusetts and New Hampshire towns used a series of trolleys to get to the park, but the rise of the automobile brought a decline to the trolley. Still, one of the few former street railway amusement resorts still in existence, continues to be popular.

Salem is home of the former Rockingham Park horse racetrack, now a multi-million dollar mixed-use property that includes retail, medical offices, condos, and apartments. The Sununu political family hails from Salem, including former New Hampshire governor and White House Chief of Staff John H. Sununu, and his sons John E. Sununu, a former U.S. senator, and current New Hampshire governor, Chris Sununu.

PEOPLE OF SIGNIFICANCE - SALEM

Katie King-Crowley (b. 1975) is an American ice hockey player from Salem. She won a gold medal at the 1998 Winter Olympics, a silver medal at the 2002 winter Olympics, and a bronze medal at the 2006 Winter Olympics.\She graduated from Brown University where she played softball and was selected as the Ivy League Softball Player of the Year in1996. At the end of her Olympic career, she ranked first all time amongst Americans in Olympic scoring with twenty-three points. In 2003, King became an assistant women's ice hockey coach for the Boston College Eagles women's ice hockey program, and was named the head coach in 2007.

Wallace Stickney (b. 1934) was an American Civil Servant, most prominently as the Director of the Federal Emergency Management Agency (FEMA) under President George H.W. Bush. Earlier in his career, Stickney worked at the U.S. Department of the Interior water division in 1968, and later became a Staff Environmental Engineer at the U.S. Environmental Protection Agency, eventually rising to the post of Environmental and Economic Office Director for U.S. Environmental Protection Agency Region One, in Boston.

Christopher Thomas Sununu (b. 1974) is an American politician and engineer. He earned his bachelor's degree in civil and environmental engineering from the Massachusetts Institute of Technology and serves as the 82nd governor of New Hampshire. Sununu is a son of former New Hampshire governor, and White House Chief of Staff John H. Sununu, and a younger brother of former U.S. representative and senator John F. Sununu.

DO YOU KNOW SALEM?

America's Stonehenge is a privately owned tourist attraction and archaeological site consisting of a number of large rocks and stone structures scattered around roughly thirty acres within the town of Salem. The site was first dubbed, "Mystery Hill", and was the official name of the site until 1982, when it was renamed, "America's Stonehenge", a term coined in a news article in the early 1960s. There are a number of hypotheses as to the origin and purpose of the structures. Some claim it has a pre-Columbian European origin, and others say that what can be seen today was created by William Goodwin, who bought the property in 1937. The area is named after Stonehenge in England, although there is no evidence of cultural or historical connection between the two.

Canobie Lake Park is an amusement park in Salem. The park's age and history inspired author Stephen King to use rides and elements from the park in his novel, "Joyland", and it is one of only 13 trolley parks still operating in the U.S. as of 2021. The park originally featured botanical gardens, with a few rides. In 1936 a wooden Roller Coaster named the Yankee Cannonball was installed, and in 1987 the Canobie Corkscrew was installed, after being relocated from the Old Chicago amusement park in Illinois, where it was named the Chicago Loop.

Today, Canobie Lake Park features a variety of rides and attractions including a water ride complex which was added in 2017, and "The Mine of Lost Souls" where passengers venture into the depths of a haunted mine. There are rides for children, for thrills, for families as well as many events held throughout the year, including live performances and fireworks shows. The park has multiple venues for live performances, including the Country Stage, Midway Stage, and Dancehall Theater. Since 1902, Canobie Lake Park has been a favorite New England attraction.

Tuscan Village is a 170-acre mix-use development project located at the former Rockingham Park Race Track site. When completed, the project is expected to offer approximately 2.8 million square feet of retail, shops, restaurants, hotels, entertainment, office space, and a variety of housing options. The development will benefit the town by generating approximately 14 million in recreation, school, public safety, and water and sewer impact fees. Additionally, the project will bring in about 5.5 million in permit fees, and $11million annually in tax revenue. It is also expected to create roughly 6,000 permanent jobs.

DERRY

ALL ABOUT DERRY

The area was first settled by Scots Irish families in 1719 as part of the town of Londonderry. The town of Derry was formed in 1827 from the eastern portion of Londonderry, and was named after the city of Derry in Ireland. The first potato planted in the United States was sown in Derry in the town's common field in 1719, and the town is the location of two of America's oldest private schools, Pinkerton Academy, founded in 1814 and still in operation, and the closed Adams Female Seminary.

Like many New Hampshire towns, Derry was once a linen and leather-making center until New England textile industries moved south in the 20th century. As recently as World War II, poet Robert Frost lived with his family on a farm in Derry purchased for him by his grandfather. The Robert Frost Farm is now a National Historic Landmark and state park and is open to the public for tours, poetry readings, and other cultural events from spring through fall.

As of 2020, Derry's population was 34,317, and covered 36.3 square miles. And although it is a town and not a city, Derry is the most populous community in Rockingham County and the fourth most populous in the state. The town's nickname, "Spacetown", derives from the fact that Derry is the birthplace of Alan Shepard, the first astronaut from the United States in space. The post-war suburban boom, and the town's proximity to Boston led to a huge population boom, but after the 1990s, this growth disappeared, with the population remaining essentially unchanged since 2000.

PEOPLE OF SIGNIFICANCE - DERRY

John Stark (b.1728) was a New Hampshire native who served in the British Army during the French and Indian War, and a major general in the Continental Army during the American Revolution. Nicknamed, "the hero of Bennington", Stark returned to military service on April 19, 1775 shortly after the Battles of Lexington and Concord, and fought brilliantly at the Battle of Bunker Hill. Washington offered Stark a command in the Continental Army where Stark and his men joined Washington's main army at the battles of Princeton and Trenton in late 1776 and early 1777.

At the pivotal battles of both Bennington and Saratoga, Stark's actions contributed to the surrender of Burgoyne's northern army for which he won promotion to brigadier general in the Continental Army. After serving with distinction throughout the rest of the war, Stark retired to his farm in Derryfield, renamed Manchester in 1810, where he died in 1822, at the age of 93.

Alan Shepard (b. 1923) was an American astronaut, naval aviator, test pilot, and businessman. After graduating from the United States Naval Academy, Shepard saw action with the surface navy during World War II. He became a naval aviator in 1946, and a test pilot in 1950. He was selected as one of the original NASA Mercury Seven astronauts in 1959, and became the person and first American, to travel into space, and the first space traveler to manually control the orientation of his craft.

In 1971, Shepard commanded the Apollo 14 mission, piloting the Apollo Lunar Module "Anteres". At age 47, he became the fifth, the oldest, and the only one of the Mercury Seven astronauts to walk on the moon. During the mission, he hit two golf balls on the lunar surface. He was promoted to rear admiral in 1971, the first astronaut to reach that rank, and retired in 1974.

Robert Frost (b. 1874) Shortly before his death, Robert Frost's grandfather purchased a farm for Robert and Elinor in Derry, where he worked for nine years while writing early in the mornings and producing many of the poems that would later become famous. His farming proved unsuccessful, and he turned to teaching English at Derry's Pinkerton Academy from 1906 to 1911, then at the New Hampshire Normal School (now Plymouth State University) in Plymouth. Although Frost lived in many different places, the Derry Farm was home from the fall of 1900 until it sold in 1911. Many of the poems in his 1916 collection, "Mountain Interval" were written at the Derry farm, and Elliot, the first son of Robert and Elinor there in 1900 at age four. The other children were educated at home by their parents.

The family moved out in the fall of 1909 to rented lodgings in Derry Village while Frost taught at Pinkerton, and by the 1940s the Frost Farm fell into disrepair. The property was purchased by the state of New Hampshire in 1964, and by 1975 the farm was open to public visitation.

Aaron Fletcher Stevens (b. 1819) was a Union Army officer during the American Civil War, and a two term U.S. Congressman. He attended Pinkerton Academy, and before the war was a machinist, lawyer, and state legislator. Stevens joined the Union Army in 1862 as colonel of the 13th New Hampshire Infantry Regiment, and saw action in the attack against Marye's Heights in the Battle of Fredericksburg. He was wounded at the Battle of Fort Harrison in 1864, and later nominated by

President Lincoln for appointment to the grade of brevet brigadier general of volunteers. Stevens served two terms in the United States House of Representatives from 1867-1871. He died in Nashua in 1887, and is buried at Universal Church Cemetery in Nashua.

David Nelson (b. 1974) is an American video game player who holds world record high scores listed in the 2008 Guinness World Records-gamer edition. As of 2008, David Nelson held more than 20 world records on arcade and console game titles. In 2005, Nelson was designated team captain of the New England Chapter of the U.S. National Video Game Team, and in 2008 was the presiding referee at the World Record Weekend Competition-an official event for inclusion in the Guinness World Records-Gamer's Edition.

Do You Know Derry?

The Adams Memorial Building, also known as the Derry Opera House, is a historic municipal building near the center of Derry. Built in 1904, it is a Colonial Revival structure. It was listed on the National Register of Historic Places in 1982, and is now operated by a local nonprofit arts organization, The Greater Derry Arts Council. It is a two-story masonry structure set on a raised basement, built out of brick with granite and wooden trim. Stone belt courses separate the first and second floors, and the second floor and the elaborate roof cornice. The main entrance is in the center bay, recessed in a round arch framed by a projecting cornice supported by clustered columns.

Taylor Mill State Historic Site is located in 71-acre **Ballard State Forest** in Derry. The site was created to protect the 1799 mill known as Taylor Up and Down Sawmill. Robert Taylor bought the land in 1799, and the mill went into operation in the 1800s. In 1939 the land was sold to Ernest Ballard, who spent two years assembling and identifying missing parts of the mill; most notable was the water wheel that he ordered from a company in Pennsylvania. In 1953, Ernest Ballard donated the mill and the land to the State of New Hampshire. The water wheel is 12 feet in diameter and 6 feet wide, and is an example of an up and down mill, which is a mechanized version of a usual saw, but was replaced by water powered circular saws around 1825.

The Robert Frost Farm in Derry is a two-story, clapboard, connected farm built in 1884 on 64 acres. It was home to Robert Frost from 1900-1911, and today is a state park in use as a historic house museum. The property, originally owned by Frost's grandfather, was declared a National Historic Landmark in 1968, and is opened to the public seasonally. Self-guided tours around the property are free, and guided tours for a nominal fee. The original soapstone sink was found in the cellar and reinstalled in the 1980s.

HAMPTON

ALL ABOUT HAMPTON

With a population of 16,214 (2020) Hampton is home to Hampton Beach, a summer tourist destination on the Atlantic Ocean coast. First called the "Plantation of Winnacunnet," Hampton was one of four original New Hampshire townships chartered by the General Court of Massachusetts, which held authority over the colony. Winnacunnet is an Algonquian Abenaki word meaning "pleasant pines" and is the name of the town's high school. The town was settled in 1638 by a group of parishioners led by Oxford University graduate Reverend Stephan Bachiler who had formerly preached at the settlement's namesake: Hampton, England. With a total area of 14.6 square miles of land, and 1.7 square miles of water, Hampton's oceanfront has always made it a popular resort, and with construction of the railroad in the 1850s its popularity grew even more.

PEOPLE OF SIGNIFICANCE - HAMPTON

Eunice Cole (b. 1950) was a woman from Hampton, better known as "Goody Cole", and is the only woman convicted of witchcraft in New Hampshire. Both she and her husband were indentured servants of Matthew Craddock, a wealthy London merchant. After their service, they came to New England and eventually moved to Hampton, receiving a 40 acre parcel of land. The 5 acre house lot was situated slightly east of where the Baptist church stands today on Winnacunnet Road.

Cole was formally accused of witchcraft three times in her life, the first in Boston in 1656 when several people testified against her. She was imprisoned until 1660, but was released in 1662. She was returned to prison until sometime between 1668 and 1671 but was eventually acquitted. She was accused again in1673, but was acquitted again in 1680, and although she was not indicted, she was still kept in prison. Upon her death in 1680, she was hastily buried in an unmarked grave.

Henry Dearborn (b. 1751) was an American military officer and politician. In the Revolutionary war he served under Benedict Arnold in his expedition to Quebec, of which his journal provides an important record. In 1775, he fought at the Battle of Bunker Hill as a captain in Colonel John Stark's 1st New Hampshire's Regiment. He served in General Washington's Continental Army, fought in the Battle of Monmouth Courthouse, and was present at the British surrender at Yorktown.

He served as Secretary of War under President Thomas Jefferson, from 1801 to 1809, and served as a commanding general in the War of 1812. Dearborn was honorably discharged from the army in 1815, was an original member of the Society of the Cincinnati and elected a member of the American Antiquarian Society in 1816, now the oldest historical society in the United States.

Jane Pierce (b. 1806), wife of President Franklin Pierce, was the first lady of the U.S. from 1853 to 1857. Born in Hampton to Reverend Jesse Appleton and Elizabeth-Means Appleton, she was the third of six children. She was shy, devoutly religious, and constantly ill from tuberculosis. She married Franklin at age 28 at her grandparents' home in Amherst, New Hampshire, though her parents were opposed to the marriage due to Pierce's political ambitions. Franklin and Jane had three sons, all of whom died in childhood, and she opposed her husband's run for the presidency, preferring a more private life. For nearly two years, she remained in the upstairs living quarters of the White House, spending her days writing letters to her dead son. By 1863, Jane's health had deteriorated and Franklin thought they should move up North hoping it would improve her condition. It did not, and Jane Pierce died of tuberculosis on December 2, 1863.

Thomas Leavitt (b. 1616) was one of the earliest permanent settlers of the Province of New Hampshire. Thomas Leavitt arrived in Boston in 1635, and an early record shows him assessed a fine. Perhaps chafing at the discipline of early Puritan Boston, Leavitt departed for Exeter in 1639, and a few years later settled in Hampton, one of the four original

New Hampshire townships chartered by the General Court of Massachusetts. Leavitt served as a selectman for Hampton in 1657, and in 1664 he served a term as constable. Thomas had four sons, all of whom lived nearby and left descendants who still reside in the area today. He died in 1696, and left 219 acres of land to his wife and children. He is buried in Pine Grove Cemetery, Hampton.

Do You Know Hampton?

The Benjamin James House is a historic house museum in Hampton. Built in 1723, it is believed to be the oldest surviving example of the traditional five-bay Georgian Colonial house, with a possibly older building attached as an ell. Now owned by a local non-profit, it's opened between May and October by appointment. The house was listed on the National Register of Historic Places in 2002. The land on which the house stands was purchased in 1705 by Benjamin James, a weaver. By 1722 James owned 30 acres, and had eight children prompting construction of the larger house the following year. The house is a 21/2 story wood frame structure, with a side-gable roof, central chimney, and clapboard exterior. The main house timbers have been dated by dendrochronology to 1723.

Hampton Beach Casino Ballroom is a live music and comedy venue located on the boardwalk of Hampton Beach. In 2010, Pollstar ranked the Casino Ballroom #23 in the Top 100 Worldwide Club Venues, and schedules upwards of 70 shows a season. The facility was opened on July 4, 1899 by Wallace D. Lovell, who owned the Exeter, Hampton and Amesbury Street Railway Company, with the hope of bringing more business and tourism into the Hampton area. After expansion, The Casino Ballroom boasted the largest dance floor in New England, and 20,000 people made use of the massive space on a weekly basis that hosted such acts as Bing Crosby and Duke Ellington. The rise of rock and roll brought more changes, and new owners sought to book such names as U2, Jerry Seinfeld, Melissa Etheridge, and Phish, and it became so popular that it was able to fit 50 events into a three-month period-unheard of at the time for most music halls. The venue's season now extends from April to November, and continues to bring in top names in entertainment.

Established in 1933, **Hampton Beach State Park** is a 50-acre state park, located on the southeastern edge of New Hampshire on a peninsula where the Hampton River meets the Atlantic Ocean. The park has a large beach, playground, amphitheater, pavilion, and first aid. Activities include swimming, fishing, picnicking, and RV camping with full hook-ups in the campground.

RYE

ALL ABOUT RYE

Like Hampton, Rye is a town in Rockingham County that is home to several state parks along the Atlantic coastline. The first settlement in New Hampshire, originally named Pannaway Plantation, was established in 1623 at Odiorne's Point by a group of fishermen led by David Thompson. The settlement was abandoned in favor of Strawberry Banke, which later became Portsmouth. Prior to its incorporation in 1726 as a parish of New Castle, Rye was called "Sandy Beach" and its lands were part of New Castle, Portsmouth, Greenland, and Hampton. In 1726, the town of New Castle set off a parish for Sandy Beach called "Rye", for Rye in Sussex, England, the ancestral lands of the Jenness family who continue to live in the town to this day, and even have a beach named after them.

Currently, the town has a population of 5,543 as of the 2020 census, and has a total area of 36.8 square miles, of which 12.6 square miles are land and 24.1 square miles are water. Rye is located on the shore of the Atlantic Ocean and includes four of the nine islands known as the Isles of Shoals, which lie approximately ten miles out from the mainland. The state parks along the Atlantic shoreline include: Jenness State Beach, Rye Harbor State Park, Wallis Sands State Beach, and 135 acre Odiorne Point State Park, home to the Seacoast Science Center.

PEOPLE OF SIGNIFICANCE - RYE

William Berry (b. 1610) was the first settler at Sandy Beach in Rye. He was in the service to Captain John Mason in 1631, when Mason sent 58 men and 22 women to the Piscataqua River in North America. He married Jane Hermins in 1636 in the town of Portsmouth, became a freeman in May of 1642 in Newbury, Massachusetts, and is on the list of the first settlers of Newbury. He received a lot of land on the south side of the Little River at Sandy Beach in 1648, which included the area where "Locke's Neck" is located.

Herbert Arthur Philbrick (b. 1915) was an advertising executive who was encouraged by the FBI to infiltrate the Communist Party USA between 1940 and 1949. His autobiography was the basis for the 1950s television series "I Led Three Lives". Philbrick's involvement began when he joined the Cambridge Youth Council, a Communist front group in Cambridge, Massachusetts. Philbrick contacted the FBI, and they encouraged him to deepen his involvement in their Communist activities. During his time in the Communist Party, its membership and support were eroded by the party's sharp zigzag from anti-war agitation during the Molotov-Ribbentrop Pact, to enthusiastic support for the war effort after the Nazi invasion of the Soviet Union.

Philbrick's career came to an end when the Justice Department decided to use him as a witness in the Smith Act prosecutions of the leadership of the Communist Party, in the Foley Square Trial. The trial took almost a year, and all 11 defendants were convicted.

Later in life, Philbrick retired to the Little Boar's Head district of North Hampton where he gave speeches, and encouraged youth to exercise their political rights and power. He died on August 16, 1993. His personal papers were acquired by the Manuscript Division of the Library of Congress, where they are made available to researchers.

DO YOU KNOW RYE?

The Elijah Locke House is one of the oldest surviving buildings in New Hampshire's Seacoast region, and is listed on the National Register of Historic Places. Constructed in 1739, it stands in a rural residential setting in central southern Rye. It is a 2 1/2-story wood-frame structure, with a side gable, center chimney, and clapboard exterior. Captain John Locke was one of the earliest settlers of New Hampshire, arriving in 1744. This house was built by either his son in 1729, or his grandson in 1739, the later date is found incised on one of the original roof beams. John Locke was killed by Native Americans in 1696, but the house spent many years in (and out of) ownership by Locke's descendants.

115

Pulpit Rock Tower is a historic military observation tower, built in 1943 as part of the Harbor Defenses of Portsmouth. It is the only one of fourteen World War II-era observation posts to survive. Located in northern Rye, on a small state-owned parcel of land, it is accessed via a footpath from Neptune Drive. It is a concrete structure standing eight stories in height. Its walls are twelve inches thick, and its floors are twelve inches thick. The interior has a six-level spiral staircase, and the tower's top two levels are accessed by wooden ladders, with an observation platform at the top. It was built by the Army Corps of Engineers, and was the only tower of its type built on the New Hampshire seacoast. The tower is now owned by the state of New Hampshire.

The Beach Club was built in 1882, and has been repeatedly modified since then. It consists of a cluster of four buildings around a saltwater swimming pool on the beach. Surrounding the pool are three bathhouses, which house changing rooms and service equipment for the pool. On the east side of the pool is a covered cabana-like area with views of the ocean It was originally run as a concession to all local visitors, but in 1925 became a private club, catering to the elite of New Hampshire and Massachusetts, who felt their summer resort being overrun by a more transient type of visitor. The original pool was built in 1927 by the club and was replaced in 2007 and now features an underwater lighting system that is a near replica of the one the original pool had.

Odiorne State Park is a 333-acre public recreation area on the Atlantic seacoast in Rye. It features the **Seacoast Science Center** and the remains of the World War II **Fort Dearborn.** The point got its name from the Odiorne family who settled the land in the mid-1660s. The park is the site of the former **Pannaway Plantation,** the first European settlement in New Hampshire, commemorated by a memorial park.

SEABROOK

ALL ABOUT SEABROOK

Seabrook is the first town one encounters when entering New Hampshire northbound on I-95. It is a town in Rockingham County located at the southern end of the coast of New Hampshire, with a population of 8,401 at the 2020 census. Seabrook is noted as the location of the

Seabrook Station Nuclear Power Plant, the third-most recently constructed nuclear power plant in the United States. The town has a total area of 9.7 square miles, of which 9.0 square miles are land, and 0.73 square miles are water.

Due to its location on the New Hampshire-Massachusetts border, Seabrook has many fireworks and firework supply stores; consumer fireworks are legal in New Hampshire, but illegal in Massachusetts and Massachusetts State Police have entered New Hampshire in an effort to crack down on the transport of fireworks over the border.

PEOPLE OF SIGNIFICANCE - SEABROOK

Scotty Lago (b. 1987) is an American snowboarder, and a 2004 world quarterpipe champion and winner of a bronze medal at the 2010 Winter Olympics with a score of 42.8 out of 50. Lago has been riding since 1996. He has raised money for the Floating Hospital in Boston, and when not snowboarding enjoys hunting and fishing. He is also a member of Friends Crew, a group of riders who turned their initial friendship into a formal alliance in 2007 to move the sport away from its recent competitive and business focus and return it to its collegial beginnings.

Meshech Weare (b. 1713) was an American farmer, lawyer, and revolutionary statesman from Seabrook. He served as the first president of New Hampshire. Before 1784, the position of governor was referred to as "president of New Hampshire". The site of his home was originally in the Third Parish of New Hampshire, now Seabrook, though the actual house burned down in the early 1900s. Weare graduated from Harvard College in 1735, and in 1739 he became a town moderator. For the next 35 years he served in various political positions. In September 1772, Weare served as one of four judges in the trial of the participants in the Pine Tree Riot, an early act of rebellion against British authority in the Colonies, and Weare was a leader in the drafting of New Hampshire's first formal constitution, the first American state to do so.

The New Hampshire town of Weare (formerly Hale's town of Robie's town) was renamed in 1764 to honor his service as the town's first clerk. In Hampton Falls, a park built in the early 2000s directly next to his house, is named for him. His grave is located in a small cemetery an eighth of a mile down the road.

Do You Know Seabrook?

The Seabrook Nuclear Power Plant, more commonly known as Seabrook Station, is a nuclear power plant in Seabrook, approximately forty miles north of Boston, and 10 miles south of Portsmouth. It has been operated since 1990, and Seabrook unit 1 is the largest individual electrical generating unit on the New England power grid. It has a 1,244-megawatt electrical output, and is the second largest nuclear plant in New England. Construction plans were finalized in 1972.

Construction began in 1976 with cooperation amongst sixteen utility groups, however, numerous problems led to construction delays, and the Three Mile Island accident in 1979 diminished outside interest in financing and buying ownership of Seabrook Station. The construction of Seabrook was completed ten years later than expected with a cost approaching $7 billion.

Numerous financial and regulatory issues have plagued the plant, and pending the resolution of current disputes, the required upgrades would be completed during the next planned refueling shutdown in 2023.

In 2013, the Nuclear Energy Institute released a study showing the positive impact of Seabrook on the economy. Key findings listed:

- Seabrook Station directly employs 650 people who earn more than double the average salary o workers in Rockingham County.
- Seabrook Station generates approximately 40 percent of New Hampshire's total electricity, and its emission –free operation helps avoid the emission of nearly 4 million tons of carbon dioxide annually.
- Seabrook Station contributes $535 million dollars of economic activity locally, and contributes $1.4 billion to the U.S. economy each year.
- Seabrook Station's financial contributions to local environment groups over the previous decade have amounted to more than $1 million.
- If the electricity generation of Seabrook Station were to be matched by wind or solar power, the required land would need about 290 square miles of wind turbines, and about 80 square miles of solar panels.

STRAFFORD COUNTY

Strafford County is in southeastern New Hampshire, with a total area of 384 square miles, the smallest county in New Hampshire by area. It's separated from York County, Maine by the Salmon Falls River. As of the 2020 census, the population was 130,889, and its county seat is Dover. The county was organized at Dover in 1771. Strafford County was one of the five original counties identified for New Hampshire in 1769, and named after William Wentworth, 2nd Earl of Strafford in the mistaken belief that he was the ancestor of governor John Wentworth-although they were distantly related, William had no descendants. There are 45 properties and districts listed on the National Register, in Strafford County, including one National Historic Landmark

DOVER

ALL ABOUT DOVER

Dover is the largest city in the New Hampshire Seacoast Region, and the fifth largest municipality in the state. Its population in 2020 was 32,741, and it covers 29.04 square miles. The first known European explorer to the region was Martin Pring from Bristol, England in 1603. In 1623, William and Edward Hilton settled at Pomeroy Cove on Dover Point, making Dover the oldest permanent settlement in New Hampshire, and seventh in the United States. The Hiltons were fishmongers sent from London by the Company of Laconia to establish a colony and fishery on the Piscataqua River. In 1631, however, it contained only three houses; William Hilton built a salt works on the property. Their name survives at Hilton Park on Dover Point, where the brothers settled near the confluence of the Bellamy and Piscataqua rivers.

The town was called Dover in 1637 by the new governor, Reverend George Burdett. It was possibly named after Robert Dover, an English lawyer who resisted Puritanism. Settlers built fortified log houses called "garrisons", inspiring Dover's nickname "The Garrison City"., and the population and business center shifted from Dover Point to Cochecho Falls on the Cochecho River, where the drop of 34 feet provided water power for industry. What is now downtown Dover, settlers called Cochecho village.

On June 28, 1689, Dover suffered an attack by Native Americans. Fifty-two colonists, a quarter of the population, were either captured or slain in a revenge attack for an incident in 1676 where Native Americans were tricked and subsequently hanged or sold into slavery. Incursions against the town would continue for the next half-century.

Cochecho Falls brought the Industrial Revolution to 19th century Dover in a big way. Expansive brick mills were constructed downtown, linked to receive cotton bales and ship finished cloth when the railroad arrived in 1842. Incorporated as a city in 1855, Dover for a time became the leading producer of textiles, the mill complex dominating the river-front and employing 2,000 workers. With the closing of the mills, the downtown area of Dover sat vacant.

At the turn of the century, the city government began to revitalize the area. The Children's Museum of New Hampshire was brought into a disused mill building, waterfront property was now used for parks and playgrounds, small businesses moved into the mills such as restaurants, barber shops, toy stores, real estate offices, and old buildings have been refurbished or rebuilt to provide new housing.

PEOPLE OF SIGNIFICANCE - DOVER

Joseph C. McConnell (b. 1922) was a United States Air Force fighter pilot who was the top flying ace during the Korean War. He was credited with shooting down 16 Mig-15s, and was awarded the Distinguished Service Cross, Silver Star, and the Distinguished Flying Cross for his actions in aerial combat. McConnell was the first American triple jet-on-jet fighter ace, and still is the top- scoring American jet ace.

Richard O'Kane (b. 1911) was a U.S. Navy submarine commander in World War II, who was awarded the Medal of Honor for commanding the USS Tang in the Pacific War against Japan to the most successful record of any U.S. submarine ever. He also received three Navy Crosses and three Silver Stars, for a total of seven awards. O'Kane retired from active duty in 1957 with the rank of rear admiral on the Retired list. In 1998, the Arleigh Burke-class destroyer USS O'Kane (DDG-77) was named in his honor. Both he and his wife are buried at Arlington National Cemetery, in Arlington, Virginia.

Jessica Parratto (b. 1994) is an eight-time USA Diving National Champion in women's platform and platform synchro. At age 17 she competed at her first world event, the 2015 World Aquatics Champion-ship. She placed 10th in the women's 10m platform at the 2016 Summer Olympics in Rio. She competed in the2020 Summer Olympics in the women's synchronized platform, placing second and winning the first-ever Olympic medal for the United States in that event.

Marilla Marks (Young) Ricker (b. 1840) was a suffragist, philan-thropist, lawyer, and freethinker. She was the first female lawyer from New Hampshire, and paved the way for women to be accepted into the

121

bar in New Hampshire. She was also the first woman to run for governor in the state, and the first to apply for a federal foreign ambassadorship post. She made significant and lasting contributions to the issues of women's rights through her actions and writings. She was educated at Colby Academy in New London, New Hampshire, and her father, Jonathan, taught her to think independently and be curious, taking her to town meetings and courtrooms. During the Civil War Marilla offered her services as a nurse for the Union Army, but she was turned down due to her lack of medical training. Instead, she devoted time and money sending clothes and other goods to aid the war effort.

By the time of the war she had become a teacher in both Lee and Dover. She refused, however, to read from the Bible preferring instead the literary works of Emerson, and left the teaching profession. In 1869, after the death of her husband Ricker attended the first National Woman Suffrage Association convention, which marked a new period of active suffragist work in her life. She attempted to vote in her hometown of Dover in 1870-the first woman to do so, and continued for decades until the end of her life.

George H. Wadleigh (b. 1842) served in the United States Navy during the American Civil War and the Spanish-American War. Wadleigh graduated the U.S. Naval Academy in 1860, and served during the Civil War in the Gulf of Mexico, seeing action at the battle of Mobile Bay. Promoted to commander in 1880, he commanded the "Alliance" during an arduous Arctic cruise searching for survivors of the ill-fated Jeannette expedition. He achieved the rank of rear admiral in 1902 and was briefly Commandant of the Philadelphia Navy Yard and President of the Board of Inspection and Survey before retiring from active duty. He died in Dover on July11, 1927. The destroyer USS Wadleigh (DD-689) was named in honor of Rear Admiral Wadleigh.

Do You Know Dover?

First Parish Church in Dover was designed and built by Captain James Davis in 1825 and is the fifth home to a parish that was first gathered in 1633 at Dover Point, and is the oldest in the state of New Hampshire. The church was added to the National Register of Historic Places in 1982, and is affiliated with the United Church of Christ. It is a tall, single-story masonry structure, built with load-bearing brick walls and a gabled roof with a stepped gable end at the front. The tower rises to include a square clock stage and an open octagonal belfry topped by a lantern stage and steeple.

The Woodman Institute Museum is a museum dedicated to history, science, and the arts. It was created in 1915 with a bequest of $100,000 from philanthropist Annie Woodman to encourage the city's education in those fields. The institute opened in 1916 under the name of "Woodman Institute", and in 1980 was placed on the National Register of Historic Places.

The museum's campus now includes three brick houses of Federal Style architecture, one of which is the former home of noted abolitionist Senator John P. Hale. Inside are exhibits of natural history, art, antiques, and local history. One famous item is the saddle in which President Lincoln rode to review troops shortly before his assassination. Also on the grounds is the 1675 William Damm Garrison House, one of the oldest intact garrison houses in the state, as well as the oldest house in Dover, and a brass Napolean cannon used in the Civil war, one of only 10 in existence. The museum's 106th season runs from April through November.

Hilton Point Park is technically the oldest continually occupied spot in the state. Originally, the Hilton brothers were granted a patent to set up a fishing company on the site, and now the site is among the most scenic in the region. There's parking for boaters, picnickers, hikers, and tourists, but because of dangerous currents there is no swimming.

Garrison Hill Tower is a 76-foot metal tower sitting on an elevation of 298 feet with wooden stairs and platforms. From earliest times, this hill was a signaling site for Native Americans. The first wooden observatory was built here in 1880. The city of Dover purchased the 8-acre hill in 1888, and the tower was built in 1913. There are no major buildings nearby, and with a 360-degree view, on a clear day visitors can see both the Isle of Shoals and the White Mountains, and is the best place to take in the entire seacoast region.

DURHAM

ALL ABOUT DURHAM

With a population of 15,490 at the 2020 census, and an area of 27.4 square miles, Durham, New Hampshire is home to the University of New Hampshire. English settlers first colonized the region in 1622 when King James I granted Sir Fernando Gorges and John Mason a vast tract of land, and colonists arrived in the same year. They spent their early years fishing, cutting and trapping to sell salted fish, lumber, and fur to European markets, and by1633, colonists were spread along the tidal shores of the Oyster River. Colonial Durham was first known as the Oyster River Plantation. Oyster River was part of Dover throughout its first century, but was granted rights as an independent parish in 1716 and incorporated as a township in 1732 when it was renamed Durham.

Benjamin Thompson, a descendant of an early settler, bequeathed his assets and family estate, Warner Farm, to the state for the establishment of an agricultural college. Founded in 1866 in Hanover, the New Hampshire College of Agricultural and the Mechanic Arts moved to Durham in 1893 and became the University of New Hampshire in 1923. Thompson Hall, built in 1892 with an iconic clock tower, is named in his honor. Designated in the Romanesque Revival Style, it was listed on the National Register of Historic Places in 1996.

In 2017, Durham became the first community in New Hampshire to recognize Indigenous People's Day in place of Columbus Day.

PEOPLE OF SIGNIFICANCE - DURHAM

Samuel Babson Fuld (b. 1981) is an American former professional baseball outfielder, and current general manager of the Philadelphia Phillies. He played eight seasons in Major League Baseball. He began his career by twice batting .600 in high school, during which time Baseball America ranked him 19th in the country. He played college baseball at Stanford University where he was a two-time All-American, and set the school record for career runs scored, and established the College World Series record for career hits.

Daphne Joyce Maynard (b.1953) is an American novelist and journalist. She began her career in journalism in the 1970s writing for Seventeen Magazine and the New York Times. Her first novel, *Baby Love,* came out in 1981, and her second novel, To Die For, in 1992, drawing on the Pamela Smart murder case, and was adapted into the 1995 film by the same name. Maynard received significant media attention in 1998 with the publication of her memoir, *At Home in the World*, which deals with her affair with J.D. Salinger. Her sixth novel, *Labor Day*, was adapted into the 2013 film of the same name, directed by Jason Reitman. In 1996, she helped lead the opposition to the construction of the nation's first high level nuclear waste dump in her home state of New Hampshire.

Daniel Chapman Stillson (b. 1826) was an American inventor who invented the adjustable pipe wrench. Born in Durham in 1826, he was a machinist during the American Civil war and served on David Glasgow Farragut's first voyage as a vice admiral. It was while working as a machinist at J.J. Walworth Company in Cambridge, Massachusetts that he developed his pipe wrench. On September 13, 1870, he was issued his patent. He was paid about $80,000 in royalties during his lifetime.

Maj. General John Sullivan (b. 1740) was a Revolutionary patriot, soldier, politician, and first Grand Master of Masons in New Hampshire. He left the Continental Congress to serve under Washington from Cambridge to Valley Forge. After retiring from the army, he re-entered Congress, then served three terms as Governor of New Hampshire. He led the fight for ratification of the U.S. Constitution, and became a federal district judge.

Do You Know Durham?

On July 18, 1694, a force of about 250 Indians under the command of the French soldier, de Villieu, attacked settlements in the area on both sides of the Oyster River, killing or capturing approximately one hundred settlers, destroying five garrison houses, and numerous dwellings. It was the most devastating French and Indian raid in New Hampshire during King Williams War. The settlement eventually rebuilt, and was protected by troops from Massachusetts.

Packer's Falls on the Lamprey River, once provided waterpower and industry for the early settlers. A deed dated 1694, shows Captain

Packer was one of a group who were granted the rights to build mills or sawmills. Today it is a popular swimming and fishing spot.

Three Chimney's Inn, and frost Sawyer Tavern were built in 1649 overlooking the Oyster River and Old Mills Falls. The Inn's seacoast location is only an hour from Boston, and a gateway to the Lakes Region and the White Mountains.

The UNH Observatory is an astronomical observatory owned and operated by the University of New Hampshire in Durham. The main telescope is a 14-inch Schmidt-Cassegrain reflecting telescope donated to the university in 1984. The observatory hosts free public sessions as well as free private sessions by advance appointment.

The John Sullivan House was the home of American Revolutionary War General John Sullivan (b. 1740). The house is located in the oldest part of Durham, now a historic district. It's a two-story L-shaped wood frame Georgian structure, with a central chimney and a gable roof. There are three bedrooms on the second floor, and much of the original woodwork dates back to the 18th century. The house was declared a National Historic Landmark in 1972, and is now a private residence.

WHAT IS THE NAME OF THIS BUILDING ON THE UNH CAMPUS?
Thompson Hall

ROCHESTER

ALL ABOUT ROCHESTER

Rochester was once inhabited by Abenaki Indians from the Pennacook tribe. They hunted, fished, and farmed, moving locations when their agriculture exhausted the soil. The town was one of four granted by colonial governor Samuel Shute of Massachusetts. Incorporated in 1722, hostility with the Abenaki people delayed settlement until 1728. It was named for his close friend, Lawrence Hyde, 1st Earl of Rochester, brother-in-law to King James II. Early dwellings clustered together for protection, but due to warfare or disease, after 1749 Native American numbers dwindled. In 1737, the Reverend Amos Main became the first pastor of the Congregational Church, located on Rochester Hill. By 1738, the farming community contained 60 families, and by 1780 the area around the Common was the most thickly settled part of town. A bandstand was constructed in 1914, and today the Common is used for community activities and concerts throughout the summer months. During the Revolutionary War the Common was used for the meeting place for soldiers before going off to war, and is now the location of the city's Civil War monument that bears the names of the 54 men who died in the conflict.

In 1752 the first public schooling began. School lasted for 16 weeks, and the schoolmaster was paid a salary of 15 pounds and boarded with a different family each month. In 1850 the city voted to allow high schools and the funding of them. At that time school lasted for 22 weeks, though attendance was relatively low, and most dropped out before graduating.

Mail service was established in 1768, and by the 19th century the town was growing. Lumber was the first large business, soon to be overtaken by other industries. In 1806 six tanneries were operating along with a sawmill, fulling mill, and two gristmills; by the 1820s the town had a cabinetmaker and clockmaker. Rochester thrived up until the Great Depression, when many industries left for cheaper operating conditions in the South, or went bankrupt. The affluent mill era left behind fine architecture, including the Rochester Public Library, a Carnegie Library. Today, the city has a total area of 45.4 square miles, drained by the Salmon Falls, Isinglass and Cochecho Rivers, with its highest point at 581 foot Chestnut Hill. Rochester was one of New Hampshire's fastest growing cities between 2010 and 2020, and known as the Lilac City.

PEOPLE OF SIGNIFICANCE - ROCHESTER

Isaac Adams (b. 1802) was an American inventor and politician who served in the Massachusetts Senate, and invented the Adams Power Press, which revolutionized the printing industry. Adams was born in Rochester and at an early age became an operative in a cotton factory. Afterward he learned the trade of cabinet-maker, but in 1824 went to Boston and sought work in a machine shop. In 1828 he invented the Adams printing press, and it was introduced in 1830 as "Adams Power Press". By 1836 it had become the leading machine used in book printing for much of the nineteenth century, and was distributed worldwide. It substantially reduced the cost of book production, and made books more widely available.

Charles Francis Hall (b. 1821) was an American Arctic explorer, best known for his collection of Inuit testimony regarding the 1845 Franklin Expedition and the suspicious circumstances surrounding his death while leading the Polaris Expedition in an attempt to be the first to reach the North Pole. Hall returned to the ship from an exploratory sledging journey, and promptly fell ill. An exhumation of his body in 1968 revealed that he had ingested a large quantity of arsenic in the last two weeks of his life. At the time, Hall had accused several of the ship's company of having poisoned him. The official investigation ruled that Hall had died from apoplexy, but later tests on bone, fingernails, and hair showed that Hall died from large doses of arsenic. No charges were ever filed.

John Hanson Twombly (b. 1814) was a Methodist minister and the fourth president of the University of Wisconsin. He was an advocate for co-education and women's education, which led to tensions with the university, and ultimately his dismissal. Twombly was mostly self-educated, and worked through his youth. In 1843, he graduated from Wesleyan University and became a Methodist minister. He also became an overseer at Harvard College from 1855=1867, and superintendent of Charlestown, Massachusetts public schools from 1866-1870. He was elected to the University of Wisconsin-Madison in 1871 as the university's fourth president but advocated for co-education against the interests of the regents and resigned in 1874. His legacy includes his advocacy for women's education.

Do You Know Rochester?

The Rochester Museum of Fine Arts was founded in 2011 to enrich people's lives through the presentation of fine art. The museum is dedicated to the accessibility of contemporary works of art made by regionally, nationally, and internationally recognized artists. The museum is located in the Rochester Community Center and Rochester Public Library, and is operated entirely by volunteers.

Designed and built between 1881 and 1883, the **Arched Bridge** is unique in New Hampshire in having heavy brick arches faced with split granite. Its 50 foot width was exceptional for the time. The bridge was designed and built by Silas Hussey, a local quarryman and stone cutter who also designed Rochester's Civil War monument.

The Roger Allen Park & Memorial Field is known as one of the best ballparks in New England, and was developed by the citizens of Rochester on lands donated by Roger Allen. The field boasts five softball, ten baseball, five soccer, one football field for the youth of the city and the New England region.

The Rochester Opera House is an 800-seat theater in Rochester, with a unique feature of a fully moveable floor, perhaps the last of this design in existence. In 1906, money was appropriated for Rochester City Hall, which included an auditorium. Furnishing City Hall included furnishing the Opera House. City Hall was opened on Memorial Day 1908, and the dedication of the Opera House consisted of a program put on by Union veterans of the Civil War. Today, the Rochester Opera House is an official community supported organization, and has been a popular presidential stop for major candidates. It has been widely credited as the undisputed leader in the city's downtown economic revival.

LEE

ALL ABOUT LEE

Lee is a town in Strafford County with a population of 4,520 at the 2020 census, and has an area of 20.2 square miles. The town is rural farm and bedroom community, being close to the University of New Hampshire. Lee was first settled by Europeans in 1657 as part of the extensive early Dover Township. It includes the Wheelwright Pond, named for the Reverend John Wheelwright, the founder of Exeter. In 1735, Durham, which included Lee, separated from Dover. Then Lee, in turn, would separate from Durham on January 16, 1776, when it was established by Colonial Governor Benning Wentworth. It was among the last of 129 towns to receive a charter during his administration, and named for British General Charles Lee, who later joined the American Revolution.

In recent years, to preserve the rural landscape in Lee, nearly 25% of the town is either being placed under permanent conservation easements, or owned by the town. One noted site is Wheelwright Pond, the site of an early battle during King William's War. Indians, incited by the government of New France, attacked Exeter in July of 1690, and were pursued by two companies that overtook them at Wheelwright Pond. Fighting left 3 officers and 15 soldiers dead, along with many Indians.

PEOPLE OF SIGNIFICANCE - LEE

Ethan Gilsdorf (b. 1966) is an American writer, poet, editor, teacher, and journalist. Raised in Lee, he wanted to be a veterinarian, cartoonist or filmmaker. He read kids adventure books and works of fantasy and science fiction, and in middle school began to write his own "Lord of the Rings rip-offs". He received his B.A. from Hampshire College in 1989, with a focus on film, video, and creative writing. He went on to publish featured stories, essays, op-eds, and reviews on travel, arts, technology, the media and pop culture in the New York Times, The Boston Globe, and Wired. His essay, "The Day my Mother became a Stranger", published in Boston Magazine, was listed in Best American Essays as a notable essay in 2016, and his book, <u>Fantasy Freaks and Gaming Geeks</u> was named a Must-Read Book by the Massachusetts Book Awards. He has lectured at schools and universities, and at conventions worldwide. He currently lives in Providence, Rhode Island.

Robert Parker Parrott (b. 1804) was an American soldier and inventor of military ordnance. He graduated from the United States Military Academy in 1824 and assigned to the 3rd U.S. Artillery as a second lieutenant. He later moved to Washington, D.C. as Captain of Ordnance, but resigned a few months later to become superintendent of the West Point Iron and Cannon Foundry in Cold Spring, New York, with which he would be associated for the remainder of his life. In 1860, he produced the Parrott rifle, an innovative rifled cannon which was used extensively during the American Civil War.

Henry Tufts (b. 1748) grew up in Lee, where he began his criminal career at the age of 14. He started with thefts of apples, pears, cucumbers, and other fruits, and later, money. Soon he began stealing horses which he disguised by coloring them, including the theft and subsequent selling of his father's horse. In his autobiography, he goes on to list numerous thefts from silver spoons to livestock and clothes. He stole from houses and barns, usually selling the stolen objects in neighboring towns.

Tufts was first imprisoned in 1770, where he attempted his first escape by using the cell's heating fire to burn through a wooden wall of the jail. He often saw himself as the unfair victim.

He spent several years among the Abenaki Indians shortly before his final arrest in 1794 in Marblehead, Massachusetts. Sentenced to hang, his sentence was commuted to life imprisonment. After five years on Castle Island in Boston Harbor, he was transferred to the jail in Salem, before escaping again to Maine where, according to his autobiography, lived as a farmer and healer without committing any further crimes.

Do You Know Lee?

Bedrock Gardens is a 20-acre garden located on a 35-acre property in Lee, noted for its landscape design, its horticulture, and its sculpture. Bedrock Gardens was bought by its present owners in 1980, and the abandoned dairy farm came with a farmhouse built circa 1740, a historic barn, a three-hole outhouse, and 37 acres of scrub forest. Over the next thirty years, 20 acres were developed into a large ornamental garden, with a wildlife pond, perennial and shrub beds, and trails. Today it's noted for its concept of "the garden as a journey", and has been called one of the most beautiful and intriguing private landscapes in New Hampshire. In 2020, it welcomed 12,000 visitors.

Lee USA Speedway is a short track oval racetrack located in Lee. The facility opened as Lee Raceway in 1964 as a dirt tri-oval, one-third mile in length. Owner Bob Bonser paved the track a year later, and it became home to the New England Super modified Racing Association.

Purchased again in 1983, it was renamed Lee Speedway, and the track was changed to be a 3/8 oval in length. At the first event held at the reconfigured track, there were 236 entrants. Over the years, the track has hosted various events including for NASCAR. The track is a member of the New Hampshire Short Track Racing Association. Entering the 2020 season, modified stock car racing is planned, including a NASCAR Whelen Modified event.

The DeMeritt Hill Farm was founded around 1820 by the DeMeritt family as a family farm, and they owned it until sometime in the 1930s. In the 40s, the farm was changed into an apple orchard, and in the 70s the farm had one of the largest dairy herds in the area. By 2020 the farm had developed new partnerships with Haunted Overload and Stripe Nine Brewery to help create the new seasonal "Haunted Overload Pumpkin Ale", created with pumpkins picked directly from the fields of the farm. The farm host a number of events throughout the season, including Haunted Overload, voted one of the top 13 haunted attractions in the country, and winner of ABC's Great Halloween Fright Night.

SULLIVAN COUNTY

Sullivan County is a county in the southwest portion of New Hampshire, and is the second-least populous county in the state. The county covers 522 square miles, and as of 2020 had a population of 43,063 with eighty-five percent of the landscape as forestland, and twelve percent as prime farm land. Many of these 18th century farms are still in the same family. Its county seat is Newport. Sullivan County was organized at Newport in 1827 from the northern portion of Cheshire County, and named for John Sullivan (1740-1795), the Revolutionary War hero and former governor.

Sullivan County has one city and fourteen towns, and shares a thirty-six mile stretch of the Connecticut River with Vermont. Today, primary industries include manufacturing, retail, health and higher education, in addition to a variety of recreational opportunities.

SUNAPEE

ALL ABOUT SUNAPEE

After going through a number of name changes before its incorporation in 1781, the name "Sunapee" was adopted by the legislature in 1850. The town, the lake, and Mount Sunapee share the same name which comes from the Algonquian word "suna" which means goose, and "apee" which means water. The Natives called the area, "Lake of the Wild Goose" because it is shaped like a goose, with the beak being in Sunapee Harbor.

Sunapee has a population of 3,342 as of the 2020 census, and occupies 25 square miles, 4.1 square miles of those being water. Before Sunapee was a tourist attraction, it was an industrial area. One factory produced 110 clothespins a minute! After the factories faded away, the major attraction became the pristine lake, once surrounded by a number of grand hotels. Lake Sunapee is the only lake in New Hampshire with three working lighthouses, which were originally built in the 1890s, currently maintained by the Lake Sunapee Protective Association.

PEOPLE OF SIGNIFICANCE – SUNAPEE

John Henry Bartlett (b.1869) grew up in Sunapee and attended public school there through high school. He then attended Colby-Sawyer College in New London, and from 1890-1894, Bartlett attended Dartmouth College. After graduation he became a teacher in Portsmouth and studied law with Judge Calvin Page. He was admitted the bar in1898. His most successful and important case was William Turner vs. Cocheco Manufacturing Company, in which a state law was established to furnish adequate fire escapes.

In 1916, Bartlett presided over the Republican State Convention. He served in the New Hampshire State House of Representatives before being elected governor in 1918. Bartlett signed the purple lilac into law as the state flower of New Hampshire on March of 1919. In 1929, he was appointed chairman of the United States section of the International Joint Commission for the U.S. and Canada, until his retirement in 1939.

Steven Victor Tallarico (b. 1948), known professionally as Steven Tyler, is an American singer best known as the lead singer of the Boston–based rock band Aerosmith. Although born in New York City, Tyler has close ties to Sunapee. Before Aerosmith, Tyler wrote what would become one of Aerosmith's signature songs, "Dream On". In 1969, Tyler attended a local rock show in Sunapee, where he first saw future bandmates Joe Perry and Tom Hamilton. In his book, *Does the Noise in my Head Bother You?* Tyler says his father used to play the piano at a local Sunapee establishment, and he used to spend his summers in Sunapee when he was a child. He still owns a summer home in Sunapee. On September 15, 2007, at the New Hampshire International Speedway, Tyler announced the launch of Dirico Motorcycles, which are designed by Tyler, engineered by Mark Dirico, and built by AC Custom Motorcycles in Manchester, and participates in a variety of charity auctions involving motorcycles, including the Ride for Children charity.

Do You Know Sunapee?

Lake Sunapee is the fifth largest lake located entirely in New Hampshire, covering 6.5 square miles with a maximum depth of 105 feet. It contains eleven islands, and is indented by several peninsulas and lake fingers, a combination which yields a total shoreline of some seventy miles. Some local people can trace their ancestry back to the Pennacooks who hunted geese in the autumn, and fished for speckled trout using nets, weirs and spears.

Lake Sunapee was a popular vacation area long before the introduction of the automobile, and steamboat service developed to ferry passengers from the south end of the lake to cottages and resort hotels around the lake. It is not uncommon to spot a moose swimming across the lake in the morning, and nearly every year loon watchers are treated to the sight of loons arriving on Lake Sunapee and fishing en masse. Records show as many as 40 loons arriving at the same time.

Lake Sunapee has seven white sandy beaches areas, including the Mount Sunapee State Park.

135

Mount Sunapee State Park is a nearly 3,000-acre public recreation area, with an extensive trail system used for all seasons. The park's ski area is operated as Mount Sunapee Resort.

Mount Sunapee Resort dates back to the 1940s, and has expanded ever since. It has three lodges, sixty-six trails spread over 230 acres, three terrain parks, and 97% of the terrain has snowmaking installed on it. In addition to chairlift rides, the Aerial Challenge Course, mini golf, Disc Golf Rentals, and entrance to the Sunapee State Beach, the resort is home to a number of annual events.

League of New Hampshire Craftsmen was conceived in the 1920s, and by 1932, the League of New Hampshire Arts and Crafts had been established, and the first League shop was opened in Wolfeboro. The following year, the first Craftsmen's Fair was held, making it the oldest craft fair in the country. This year, the 89th Annual Craftsmen's fair will be held August 6-14 at the Mount Sunapee Resort.

CLAREMONT

ALL ABOUT CLAREMONT

With a population of 12, 949 (2020), Claremont is the only city in Sullivan County. Before colonial settlements, the Upper Connecticut River Valley was home to the Pennacook and Western Abenaki peoples. The Hunter archeological site located near the bridge connecting Claremont with Ascutney, Vermont, is a significant prehistoric Native American site that includes seven levels of occupational evidence, including evidence of at least three long houses. The oldest dates recorded from evidence gathered during excavations in 1967 were to 1300 CE.

The city has a total area of 44.1 square miles, and was named after Claremont, the country mansion of Thomas Pelham-Holles, Earl of Clare, and first settled in1762. The undulating surface of rich, gravely loam made agriculture an early occupation. In 1784, Col. Samuel Ashley was given a charter to establish a ferry across the Connecticut River, the location of which is still known as Ashley's Ferry landing.

Water power harnessed from the Sugar River brought the town prosperity during the Industrial Revolution. Many brick mills were built along the stream, and produced cotton, woolen textiles, lathes, planers, and paper, although like other New England mill towns, much industry moved away or closed in the 20th century.

PEOPLE OF SIGNIFICANCE – CLAREMONT

William Wilgus (b. 1865) was known for his prominent career in civil engineering, working on some of the largest and most complex railroad projects during his time. In 1893 he began his association with the New York Central and Hudson River Railroad, and by 1899 he became the railroad's chief engineer for construction and maintenance. He supervised the planning and construction of Buffalo Union Station, the Michigan Central Railway Tunnel, and the Weehawken Terminal. Along with Frank Sprague, he designed and patented the Wilgus-Sprague bottom contact third rail system.

Raised in Claremont, **Dorothy Loudon** (b. 1925) was an American actress and singer, who won the Tony Award for Best Lead Actress in a Musical in 1977 for her performance as Miss Hannigan in "Annie". She has many theater, film, and television credits, but appeared in only two films, playing an agent in the film, "Garbo Talks" (1984) and as Southern eccentric Serena Dawes in "Midnight in the Garden of Good and Evil".

Benjamin Tyler Henry (b. 1821) was an American gunsmith, and the inventor of the Henry rifle, the first reliable lever-action repeating rifle. Henry was born in Claremont on March 22, 1821. On October 16, 1860, he received a patent on the Henry .44 caliber repeating rifle, which proved the worth of the lever-action design in the American Civil War.

Born in Claremont, **Kaleb Tarczewski (b. 1993)** is an American professional basketball player who, for two years, led the Stevens High School varsity basketball team to the NHIAA final four. In college, the 7 foot tall center played four seasons with Arizona, where he averaged 9.4 points, 9.3 rebounds and 1.4 blocks and was named to the Pac-12 ALL-Conference Second team and the Pac-12 All-Defensive team. Tarczewski won a bronze medal at the 2015 Pan American Games.

DO YOU KNOW CLAREMONT?

The United Episcopal Church in West Claremont was built in 1773 and is the oldest surviving Episcopal church building in New

Hampshire and the state's oldest surviving building built exclusively for religious purposes.

During the American Revolution, Claremont had a large number of Loyalists, who used a small wooded valley in West Claremont called the **"Tory Hole"** to hide from the Patriots.

In the 1850s, the city of Claremont sought permission from the state legislature to build a public high school. At the time, public high schools did not exist in New Hampshire. The state agreed, resulting in **Stevens High School.**

In March 1989, the Claremont School Board filed suit against the state of New Hampshire, claiming that the state's reliance on property taxes for funding education resulted in inequitable educational opportunities. The New Hampshire Supreme Court agreed. The **"Claremont Decision"** continues to play a vital role in this legal challenge.

The Twin State Speedway is a one-third-mile semi-banked asphalt oval nestled in the woods off of Thrasher Road in Claremont. The speedway features six divisions on a weekly basis and is the only track that runs the Tour Type Modified Division in New England.

Identified in 1952, the **Hunter Archaeological Site** is a significant prehistoric Native American site in Claremont. Artifacts have been found in soils to a depth of 11 feet, and appear to represent at least seven periods of occupation. The site was listed on the National Register of Historic Places in 1976.

NEWPORT

ALL ABOUT NEWPORT

Forty-three miles west-northwest of Concord, the state capital, is **Newport,** the county seat of Sullivan County. Granted in 1753 by colonial governor Benning Wentworth, the town was named "Greenville" after George Grenville, Prime Minister of Great Britain, and brother-in-law of William Pitt. But ongoing hostilities during the French and Indian War delayed settlement until 1763, but the town was incorporated in 1761 as "Newport", for Henry Newport, a distinguished English soldier and statesman. In 1781, however, Newport joined with 33 other towns along the Connecticut River and seceded from New Hampshire to join Vermont. George Washington dissolved their union with Vermont in 1782, and the towns rejoined New Hampshire.

Newport has a population of 6,299 (2020), and a total land area of 43.64 square miles. A covered bridge is in the northwest part of town, noted for maple sugar and apple orchards. The first cotton mill was established in 1813, and local cabinet making flourished producing many pieces of fine furniture. By 1859 Newport had three woolen mills, two tanneries, and the Sibley Scythe Company, which manufactured the scythes used to clear jungle during the construction of the Panama Canal.

PEOPLE OF SIGNIFICANCE – NEWPORT

Edmund Burke (b.1809) moved to Newport in 1834, when he assumed editorial management of the *New Hampshire Argus*, and merging with the New *Hampshire Spectator.* The newly created, *Argus and Spectator* was a political newspaper. Burke served as a United States Representative for the State of New Hampshire, and in 1846 was appointed Commissioner of Patents by President Polk. After leaving office, he resumed the practice of law in Newport. Burke died in Newport in 1882, and is interred at the Maple Grove Cemetery in Newport.

David Sargent (b.1931), native of Newport, was president of Suffolk University in Boston, Massachusetts from 1989 to 2020. From 1972 to 1989, Sargent directed the law school as Dean. The Sargent building which houses Suffolk University Law School is named after him.

Sarah Josepha Hale (b.1788) was born in Newport to Captain Gordon Buell, a Revolutionary War veteran, and Martha Whittlesay Buell. In 1827, she published her first novel under the title *Northwood: Lie North and South.* The novel made her one of the first novelists to write about slavery, as well as one of the first women novelists. Hale wrote to President Lincoln to convince him to support legislation establishing a national holiday of Thanksgiving in 1863, earning her the nickname "Mother of Thanksgiving". Hale retired from editorial duties in1877 at the age of 89. The same year, Thomas Edison spoke the opening lines of "Mary had a Little Lamb" as the first speech ever recorded on his newly invented phonograph. Hale was the author of the nursery rhyme, "Mary had a Little Lamb."

Billy B. Van (b.1870) was a prominent American actor in the early decades of the 1900s. He moved to Newport around 1915, where he became a booster of Newport, and more broadly, New England. He is widely credited with coining the nickname, "The Sunshine City" for the town, which it still uses. He has been credited with being instrumental in the formation of MGM, and the Newport newspaper called him one of the most colorful citizens in its long history. Van died in a hospital in Newport in 1950, and is buried in Pine Grove Cemetery in Newport.

Do You Know Newport?

Parlin Field is a small municipal airfield located just one mile from downtown Newport. Parlin Field, in partnership with the Newport School District, hosts an Aviation Career Education Academy, which exposes students to the wide variety of aviation careers.

Opened in 1923, the **Newport Golf Course** is an 18-hole, par seventy-one course designed by George F. Sargent, Jr. Featured in Golf Magazine as a hidden gem, the course utilizes the natural beauty of the surrounding mountains, streams, and ponds to frame the eighteen holes built on 143 acres.

Pinnacle Mountain Bike Trail has been rated #15 out of 114 mountain bike trails in New Hampshire. It's a ten-mile track with many loops and short single track trails with tough technical sections, including interesting bridges, ledge steps, and winding singlet-track downhill. Trails are well marked, but not recommended for beginners.

Newport Opera House was built in1872, destroyed by fire in 1885, and rebuilt in 1886. In 1913, two 3-globe lampposts were set in front of the Opera House, the model for today's vintage lighting on Main Street. Throughout the years, the hall has been the center of community events, and in 1980 was listed on the National Register of Historic Places.

TREASURES OF NEW HAMPSHIRE

I define "Treasures" as the places, institutions, organizations that make New Hampshire an incredibly special place for millions of people. Some are well known, and others are best known only by full and part time residents. I have selected the ones that, to me, and hopefully to the reader, qualify as special. After you have experienced them, you feel a sense of admiration and wonder. People who live in or visit New Hampshire are indeed fortunate to experience these incredibly special organizations, places and institutions.

OLD MAN IN THE MOUNTAIN

The old man of the mountain was a series of five granite cliff ledges on Cannon Mountain in Franconia that appeared to be above Profile Lake, and was 40 feet tall and 25 feet wide. The first written mention of the Old Man was in 1805, and soon became a landmark and cultural icon for the state of New Hampshire. The profile has been the state's emblem since 1945, and was put on the state's license plate, state route signs, and on the back of New Hampshire's statehood quarter.

Freezing and thawing opened fissures in the profile, and by the 1920's the crack was wide enough to be mended with chains. Nevertheless, the formation collapsed to the ground between midnight and 2 a.m., May 3, 2003. Today, there is an Old Man of the Mountain Memorial on a walkway along Profile Lake below Cannon Cliff.

MOUNT MONADNOCK

Mount Monadnock is the most prominent mountain peak in Southern New Hampshire. It has often been cited as one of the most frequently climbed mountains in the world and has been featured in the writings of Ralph Waldo Emerson and Henry David Thoreau. At 3,165 feet, it offers a number of hiking trails with a barren summit largely because of fires set by early settlers. The first major fire was set in 1800 to clear the lower slopes for pasture. Between 1810-1820 local farmers, who believed wolves were denning in the blowdowns, set fire to the mountain again.

141

Loosely translated from the Abenaki, "monadnock" means "mountain that stands alone "and was the subject of one of Emerson's most famous poems. Between 1844-1860 Thoreau visited the mountain four times cataloguing natural phenomena and is regarded as having written one of the first naturalist inventories of the mountain.

MOUNT WASHINGTON COG RAILWAY

The Mount Washington Cog Railway is the world's first mountain-climbing cog railway, and the second steepest rack railway in the world. The railway is about 3 miles long, and ascends Mount Washington's western slope, beginning at an elevation of 2,700 feet above sea level and ending just short of the mountain's peak of 6,288 feet.

Construction started in 1866, and despite the railroad's incomplete state, the first paying customers started riding on August 14, 1868, and construction reached the summit in July, 1869. To date, the railway has taken more than five million people to the summit during its existence, and operations of trains all winter began in 2004-2005

LAKE WINNIPESAUKEE

Lake Winnipesaukee is the largest lake in New Hampshire, located in the lake's region at the foothills of the White Mountains. It is approximately twenty-one miles long, and from 1-9 miles wide, covering 69 square miles. The lake contains at least 264 islands, and is indented by several peninsulas, yielding a total shoreline of 288 miles. Winnipesaukee is the third largest lake in New England after Lake Champlain and Moosehead Lake.

Lake Winnipesaukee has been a popular tourist destination for over a century, with a number of communities surrounding it: **Gilford** is home to Gunstock Mountain Resort, and Bank of New Hampshire Pavilion, a popular concert venue. **Laconia** is the main commercial city on the lake and includes Weirs Beach, the largest public beach on the lake, and is home to Bike Week. **Center Harbor** is the winter home of the MS Mount Washington. **Moultonborough** is home to the Castle in the Clouds. **Wolfeboro** is billed as the "Oldest Summer Resort in America."

The lake and its surrounding area is home to numerous summer camps, theater troupes, hiking trails, resorts, offering a variety of land and water recreational activities.

APPALACHIAN TRAIL

New Hampshire has 161 miles of trail, almost all within the White Mountain National Forest. New Hampshire has more trail above the tree-line than any other Appalachian State. The trail reaches 17 of the 48 four thousand footers, including the 6,288- foot Mount Washington. The area is subject to extremes of weather with little natural shelter, and only occasional man- made shelter from the elements. The threat of severe and cold conditions across the New Hampshire section is present year-round.

DARTMOUTH COLLEGE

Dartmouth College was established in 1769, one on the nine colonial colleges chartered before the American Revolution. Although originally founded to educate Native Americans in Christian Theology, the university primarily trained Congregationalist ministers during its early history. Situated on a terrace above the Connecticut River, Dartmouth's 269 -acre main campus is in the rural, upper valley region of New England. The school is consistently cited as a leading university for undergraduate teaching and boasts many prominent alumni. The college has 39 academic departments offering 56 major programs, while students are free to design special majors or engage in dual majors. Through the Graduate Studies Program, Dartmouth grants doctorate and master's degrees in 19 Arts and Sciences graduate programs. Additionally, Dartmouth is home to three professional schools: Geisel School of Medicine, Thayer School of Engineering, and the Tuck School of Business.

MOUNT WASHINGTON HOTEL

The Mount Washington Hotel was built between 1900-1902 at a cost of $1.7 million (approximately $55.4 million today). 250 Italian artisans were brought in to build it, particularly the granite and stucco masonry. Construction started in 1900, and at its completion, the hotel boasted over 2,000 doors, 12,000 windows, and over eleven miles of plumbing.

143

The hotel is one of the last remaining grand hotels in the White Mountains, and includes a Donald Ross designed 18- hole golf course. It was declared a National Historic Landmark in 1986

NEW HAMPSHIRE MOTOR SPEEDWAY

Located in Louden, New Hampshire Motor Speedway has hosted NASCAR racing annually since 1990, as well as the longest running motorcycle race in North America-the Louden Classic. Nicknamed "The Magic Mile", the track is currently one of eight major NASCAR tracks owned and operated by Speedway Motor Sports, and is the largest speedway in New England, and further expansion has made it the largest sports and entertainment venue of any type in the region. In 2009, the track introduced its first mascot, Milo the moose. He wears a fire suit with the Speedway Motor Sports logo and is seen on race weekends shaking hands with the drivers and hanging out with the fans.

SEABROOK NUCLEAR POWER PLANT

The Seabrook Station is a nuclear power plant in Seabrook, about 40 miles north of Boston, Massachusetts. It has operated since 1990 and is the largest individual electrical generating unit on the New England power grid. With its 1,244-megawatt electrical output, Seabrook unit 1 is the second largest nuclear power plant in New England after the two-unit Millstone Nuclear Power Plant in Connecticut.

Although there has been much controversy over the plant, the Nuclear Energy Institute found that Seabrook Station: employs 650 people who earn more than double the average salary of workers in Rockingham and Strafford County; generates 40 per cent of New Hampshire's total electricity; contributes $535 million of economic activity locally; and helps avoid the emission of nearly four million tons of carbon dioxide annually.

ODIORNE STATE PARK

Odiorne State Park is a public recreation area in the town of Rye, named after the Odiorne family who settled the area in the mid-1660's. From 1942-1947, the park was the site of Fort Dearborn, part of the coastal defense system as well as a radar station for the Air Force. Today, the primary facility in the park is the Seacoast Science Center. The Center offers indoor and outdoor programs on marine life and conservation, and exhibits include aquariums, touch tanks, and whale skeletons. There are also opportunities for hiking, cycling, fishing, boating, and picnicking.

THE CURRIER

The Currier Museum of Art is an art museum in Manchester. It features European and American paintings, decorative arts, photographs and sculpture. The permanent collection includes works by Picasso, Matisse, Monet, O'Keeffe, Calder, Scheier and Goldsmith, John Singer Sargent, Frank Lloyd Wright, and Andrew Wyeth. Public programs include tours, live classical music and "Family Days" which include activities for all ages. The Museum maintains two house museums, the Zimmerman House and the Toufic H. Kalil House, both designed by architect Frank Lloyd Wright.

SYMPHONY NEW HAMPSHIRE

A celebrated source of innovation, inspiration, education, and entertainment since 1923, Symphony New Hampshire is the premiere symphony orchestra of the Granite State. From its humble beginnings over 98 years ago as a mainly all-Nashua musician group that performed two concerts each season in the City of Nashua, the orchestra has since grown into a vibrant jewel in the cultural crown of New Hampshire. Today, concerts are offered not only in Nashua, but throughout the state in large and small venues.

Recognized throughout the state, Symphony NH is known for its performances of masterworks, rare gems, contemporary compositions, pops, and popular works not only in the classical genre, but also in the jazz and pops genres. A wonderfully diverse selection of repertoire is presented in a fresh, current way, and the key elements of fun and memorable experiences are always included. Visit www.symphonynh.org.

CAN YOU IDENTIFY THIS PHOTO? The Haverhill-Bath covered bridge, believed to be the oldest covered bridge in the state, connects Woodsville to Bath in Grafton County.

CAN YOU IDENTIFY THIS PHOTO? Named Mystery Hill and commonly known as America's Stonehenge, this privately owned tourist attraction and archeological site on 30 acres is in Salem.

PHOTOS - QUESTIONS AND ANSWERS

1. **Can you name this historic site in Conway?**

2. **Can you name this grand resort?**

3. What rare document was found in the museum in 1991 and what is the name of the museum?

4. What is this memorial and where is it located?

5.   What is the name of this wall in Sandwich?

6.   What does this statue of JFK commemorate?

7. **Where was this photo taken?**

8. **Why is this building in Hillsdale famous?**

9.   **Where is this sign in Manchester?**

10.   **What is this land used for in Littleton?**

11.   What is the name of this statue and where is it located.

12.   What is unusual about what is buried beneath this gravestone?

PHOTO ANSWERS

1. The Abenaki Indian Shop and Camp is a historic Native American site in the Intervale section of Conway. The site is a camp established by Abenakis who were lured to the area by the prospect of making baskets and selling them to visitors to the White Mountain resorts in the late 19th century. The camp operated into the late 20th century.

2. The Balsams Grand Resort Hotel in Dixville Notch.

3. A rare copy of the Declaration of Independence known as a Dunlap Broadside was found in the Ladd-Gilman house, 200 years after its arrival in Exeter.

4. It is a memorial to the veterans of the Afghanistan and Iraq Wars and it is located in McGregor Park, Derry. The 9-foot-tall, 18,000 pound reflective black granite stone is engraved with the names of veterans.

5. The Great Wall of Sandwich. It is 7 feet high and runs for a mile. It took 100 laborers two years to build.

6. The statue is in front of Nashua's City Hall and commemorates the place and the day, Jan. 25, 1960, that the then Massachusetts Senator held the first stop in his campaign for president.

7. This photo was taken at the top of Mt. Monadnock in Jaffrey.

8. It houses the oldest continuously used Post Office in America.

9. The sign is over Kelly Street on the West Side of Manchester.

10. This is the Wallace Horse cemetery in Littleton. The plaque notes that the horses were buried with all of their "harnesses, bridles, blankets, and feed boxes."

11. Stone Face, at St. Anselm College in Manchester. It depicts the Greek muse of comedy.

12. This is the gravestone marking Captain Samuel Jones's amputated leg. Jones buried his leg in the town cemetery in Washington, in Sullivan County, because folklore held that to prevent feeling any pain from a missing leg, it must be buried.

Made in the USA
Middletown, DE
09 March 2023

26417437R00086